7/74 SA

Your Book of Prehistoric Britain

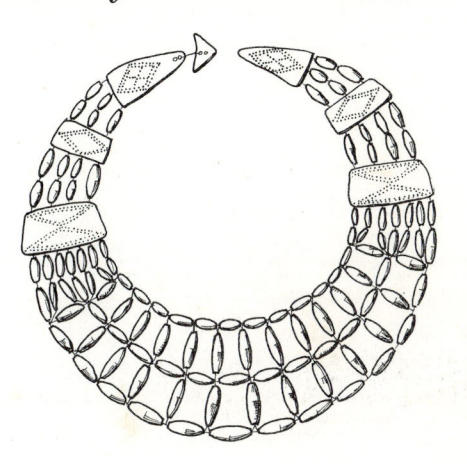

The *Your Book* Series

Acting · Aeromodelling · Animal Drawing · Aquaria · Astronomy · Badminton · Ballet · Bridges · Butterflies and Moths · Cake Making and Decorating · Camping · The Way a Car Works · Card Games · Card Tricks · Chemistry · Chess · Coin Collecting · Computers · Confirmation · Contract Bridge · Medieval and Tudor Costume · Seventeenth and Eighteenth Century Costume · Nineteenth Century Costume · Cricket · Dinghy Sailing · The Earth · Electronics · Embroidery · Engines and Turbines · Fencing · Film-Making · Fishes · Flower Arranging · Flower Making · Flying · Freshwater Life · Golf · Gymnastics · Hovercraft · The Human Body · Judo · Kites · Knitted Toys · Knitting and Crochet · Knots · Landscape Drawing · Light · Magic · Maps and Map Reading · Mental Magic · Model Car Racing · Modelling · Money · Music · Paper Folding · Parliament · Party Games · Patchwork · Patience · Pet Keeping · Photographing Wild Life · Photography · Keeping Ponies · Prehistoric Britain · Puppetry · The Recorder · Roman Britain · Rugger · The Seashore · Self-Defence · Sewing · Shell Collecting · Skating · Soccer · Sound · Space Travel · Squash · Stamps · Surnames · Survival Swimming and Life Saving · Swimming · Swimming Games and Activities · Table Tennis · Table Tricks · Tape Recording · Television · Tennis · Trampolining · Trees · Veteran and Edwardian Cars · Vintage Cars · Watching Wild Life · Waterways · The Weather · Woodwork

Your Book of
Prehistoric Britain

written and illustrated by

JAMES DYER

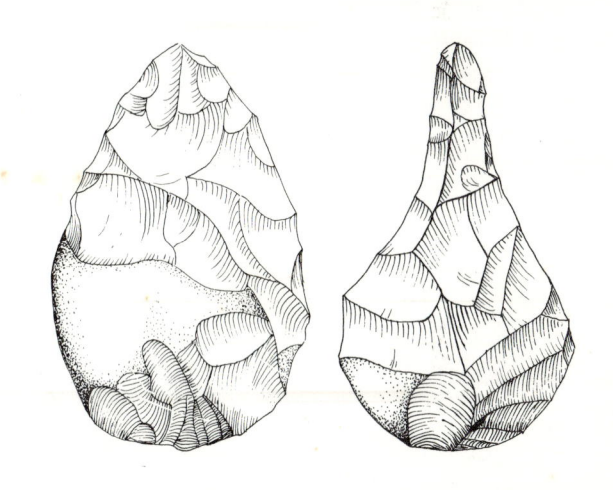

FABER AND FABER
3 Queen Square · London

*First published in 1974 by
Faber and Faber Limited
3 Queen Square London WC1
Printed in Great Britain by
Butler and Tanner Ltd
All rights reserved*
ISBN 0 571 09883 5
© *James Dyer 1974*

For Andrew and Clare Boddy

Contents

	Illustrations	8
	Acknowledgements	10
	Metric Conversion Tables and Time Chart	11
1 ·	*Archaeology and Prehistoric Times*	13
2 ·	*In the Beginning: the Old Stone Age*	18
3 ·	*Britain Becomes and Island: the Middle Stone Age*	24
4 ·	*The First Farmers: the Early Neolithic*	27
5 ·	*Religion and Burial: the Middle Neolithic*	35
6 ·	*The Beaker Folk: the Late Neolithic*	42
7 ·	*Chieftains and Peasants: the Bronze Age*	50
8 ·	*Farms and Fortresses: the Early and Middle Iron Age*	62
9 ·	*The End of Prehistoric Times: the Late Iron Age*	70
10 ·	*Some Museums and Books and You*	78
	Index	80

Illustrations

1	An early nineteenth-century excavation	12
2	A modern excavation of an Iron Age site	14
3	Equipment used for radiocarbon dating	15
4	Simple stratification	16
5	An aerial photograph of 'crop-marks'	17
6	The approximate length of the Ice Ages	19
7	An Acheulean hand-axe in use	20
8	Acheulean hand-axes	21
9	Typical microliths	25
10	A reconstructed polished-stone axe	28
11	Polished-stone axes in use to chop down a tree	28
12	The ridgeways of Southern Britain	29
13	Inside a flint mine on Harrow Hill in Sussex	31
14	One of the Harrow Hill flint mines	32
15	The distribution of stone axes	33
16	Early Neolithic pottery	34
17	An Early Neolithic bowl and a Late Neolithic pot	34
18	The henge monument of Avebury in Wiltshire	36
19	The West Kennet long barrow	38
20	Inside the West Kennet long barrow	39
21	Wayland's Smithy	40
22	The passage grave of Bryn Celli Ddu	41
23	Interior of a hut at Skara Brae in the Orkneys	43
24	Late Neolithic crouched burial	44
25	A bell-beaker and a long-necked beaker	44
26	Typical contents of a Beaker grave	45
27	The Heel Stone at Stonehenge	47
28	The bluestone Stonehenge in Period 2	47
29	An aerial view of Stonehenge	47
30	Bronze Age round barrows, Taphouse, Cornwall	48
31	The stone circle at Castlerigg near Keswick	49
32	Bronze Age pottery	50
33	The Rillaton gold cup	51
34	The Bush Barrow mace, or sceptre	51
35	Types of Bronze Age round barrows	52
36	Construction details of lintels at Stonehenge	52
37	The great sarsen stone circle at Stonehenge	53
38	A Bronze Age skull showing trepanning operations	54
39	Reconstruction of a Bronze Age family group	55
40	An amber necklace and a gold lunula	56

41	The Middle Bronze Age farm on Itford Hill, Sussex	57
42	A saddle quern and a rotary quern	58
43	Bronze Age metalwork: daggers and spearheads	60
44	The development of bronze axes	61
45	A hillfort palisade	64
46	A hillfort entrance	65
47	The banks and ditches of Maiden Castle	66
48	Contour and promontory hillforts	67
49	A chariot burial from Yorkshire	69
50	The engraved back of a Late Iron Age bronze mirror	70
51	A Late Iron Age bronze chariot-fitting	71
52	An iron firedog from a rich chieftain's grave	71
53	Map of the Iron Age tribes of Britain	72
54	Wheelmade Belgic pottery	73
55	An Iron Age chariot	74
56	Coins of Cunobelin and Verica	74
57	The Broch of Mousa in Shetland	76
58	A Late Iron Age village at Chysauster near Penzance	77

Acknowledgements

I should like to thank Nicholas Thomas, Gwyn Morgan and Richard Porter for reading this book in manuscript and making many valuable suggestions. A number of young people were helpful in the preparation of photographs and I am particularly indebted to Stephen Burke, Gregory Dale, Alastair and Christopher Fadden, Andrew Morgan, Mark Taylor and Patrick Tyrrell. I have also received much help in the production of photographs from Kenneth Annable, Arnold Baker (5, 29), R. A. Gardner (56) and Joseph Hughes (31). The British Museum (3) Colchester Museum (54, 56), Devizes Museum, Letchworth Museum (52), Leicester Museum (39), the Forhistorisk Museum at Moesgaard, Denmark (10, 11), the Sussex Archaeological Society (13) and the Department of the Environment (23, 49 Crown Copyright) have also readily supplied me with prints, or allowed me to photograph material in their collections.

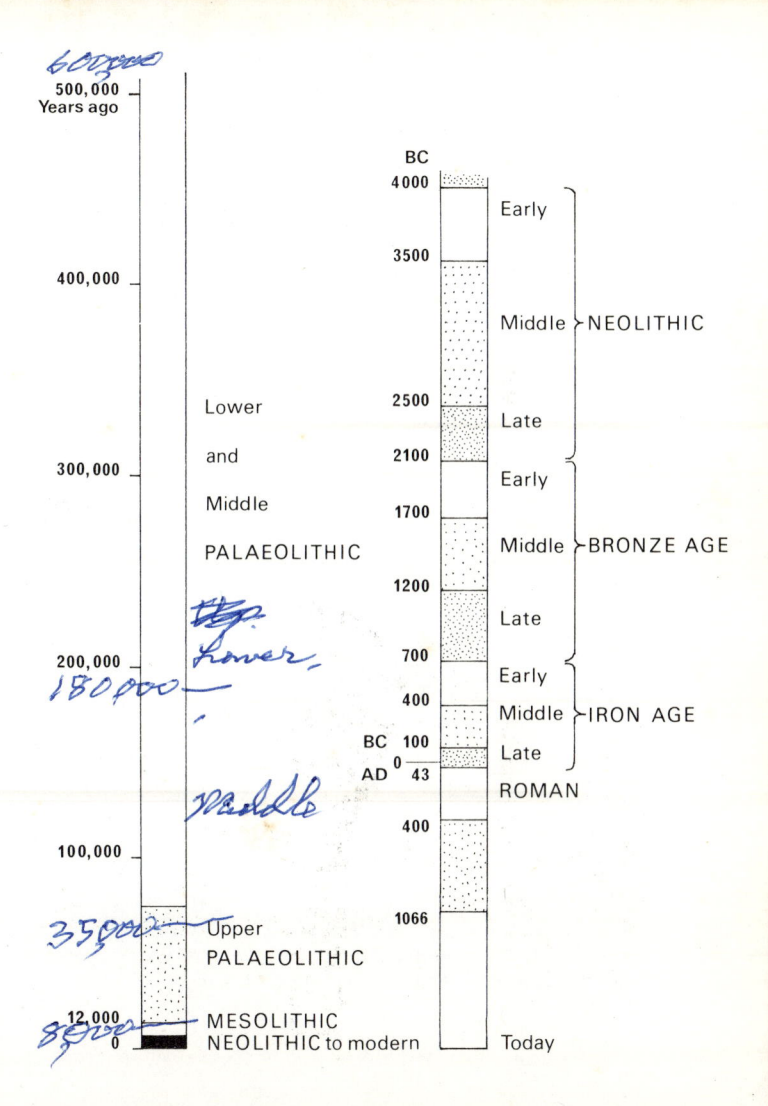

Metric Conversion Tables and Time Chart

The bold figures in the central columns can be read as either the metric or the British Measure. For example 1 inch = 2.54 centimetres; or 1 centimetre = 0.39 inches.

cms		inches	metres		feet	metres		yards
2.54	1	0.39	0.30	1	3.28	0.91	1	1.09
5.08	2	0.79	0.61	2	6.56	1.83	2	2.19
7.62	3	1.18	0.91	3	9.84	2.74	3	3.28
10.16	4	1.57	1.22	4	13.12	3.66	4	4.37
12.70	5	1.97	1.52	5	16.40	4.57	5	5.47
15.24	6	2.36	1.83	6	19.69	5.49	6	6.56
17.78	7	2.76	2.13	7	22.97	6.40	7	7.66
20.32	8	3.15	2.44	8	26.25	7.32	8	8.75
22.86	9	3.54	2.74	9	29.53	8.23	9	9.84
25.40	10	3.94	3.05	10	32.81	9.14	10	10.94

km		miles
1.61	1	0.62
3.22	2	1.24
4.83	3	1.86
6.44	4	2.49
8.05	5	3.11

Years ago
500,000
400,000
300,000
200,000
100,000

Lower and Middle PALAEOLITHIC

Upper PALAEOLITHIC — 35,000

MESOLITHIC — 12,000
NEOLITHIC to modern — 0

BC
4000 — Early
3500 — Middle ⎱ NEOLITHIC
2500 — Late
2100 — Early
1700 — Middle ⎱ BRONZE AGE
1200 — Late
700 — Early
400 — Middle ⎱ IRON AGE
BC 100 — Late
AD 0
43 — ROMAN
400
1066
Today

1 An early nineteenth-century excavation. A water colour drawing by Philip Crocker of a round barrow being excavated by William Cunnington and Sir Richard Colt Hoare

1 · *Archaeology and Prehistoric Times*

Historians write history books by using written records. Archaeologists write prehistory by trying to reconstruct what life was like from the objects that man left behind him. Prehistory is the time from the very first men on earth to the beginning of writing. Written history starts at different times in every civilization. In Egypt it began about 3100 BC, but in southern Britain it did not begin until the Romans arrived in AD 43, and in Scotland it was almost forty years later. From archaeology we can get a good idea of how man lived and died, but we can tell little about what he thought or felt. Imagine an archaeologist of the future trying to tell what kind of family yours was, by examining only the rubbish in your dustbin!

People in the past have often recognized ancient sites and sometimes explained them as the work of the devil, the little people or the supernatural. Since the seventeenth century more accurate information has been recorded by people like John Aubrey and William Stukeley, who travelled about Britain writing down and drawing the ancient places that they saw. In the nineteenth century archaeology became a fashionable hobby for country gentlemen who particularly enjoyed digging into barrows or burial mounds. Sir Richard Colt Hoare and William Cunnington in Wiltshire (Fig. 1), Thomas Bateman in Derbyshire, Canon Greenwell and J. R. Mortimer in Yorkshire, each established a reputation as barrow diggers who worked with reasonable care for their day, though by modern standards they were little more than tomb plunderers. Fortunately they did record and keep what they found. So unscientific was some of the work that went on at that time that as many as thirty barrows might be dug into in a single day. Nowadays we would consider a month a more reasonable time to examine a single burial mound.

Whilst these people dug, others collected ancient objects and our first museums began. At the same time canals and railways were being built; huge quantities of earth were dug up and the workmen unearthed innumerable objects. These were stored in crowded cases and, since no one had much idea of their age, were labelled 'Ancient British', 'Celtic' or 'Pictish'.

It was a Danish archaeologist, Christian Thomsen, the first curator of the National Museum in Copenhagen in 1816, who first put some order into these objects by sort-

2 A modern excavation of an Iron Age site. You should be able to make out the stratification of the ditch quite clearly.

ing the cutting tools, like axes and knives, into groups belonging to the three ages which, he believed, had followed after each other. The first he called the Stone Age. This, he said, was when men used stone for their tools and weapons, but knew nothing of metal; the second was the Bronze Age, in which they used only copper and bronze, and the third the Iron Age, in which they used iron as well as the rest. In a sense we still live in the Iron Age today. It was left to Thomsen's pupil Jan Worsaae to excavate in the Danish peat bogs and burial mounds and prove that this order was correct.

Although the nineteenth-century diggers found lots of objects for museums, the rough and ready way in which they dug gave little information about the earthworks in which they were found or the people who made them. A scientific approach was needed, and it came in the 1880's with Lieutenant-General Pitt-Rivers. The General conducted excavations like a military campaign. The site was carefully surveyed before digging began, and then as it was excavated the position of every flint, piece of pottery and bone was accurately recorded. After the site had been totally uncovered a meticulous report was published giving detailed plans and descriptions, from which it is still possible to reconstruct a picture of everything that was found. The General made it clear that an excavation can never be repeated. Once the site has been dug it has been destroyed for ever, so every possible detail must be observed at the time and an account printed so that anyone can read about it.

It is these principles and ideas of Pitt-Rivers that still guide archaeologists today. Of course there have been new ideas since his time, but we still believe that an excavation must be carried out as carefully as a surgical operation, and that it should only be done by skilled and trained workers (Fig. 2).

By combining our knowledge of museum objects with skilled excavation we can build up a picture of the life of prehistoric man, although he left no writing to tell us about it.

Even though pottery and tools in a museum may have been found a long time ago they can still give us new information about the past. A thin slice cut from a stone axe and placed under a microscope can tell us where the stone came from; similarly a fine slice of pottery can tell us the source of the clay from which it was made. From this we can discover whether the objects were made close to the place where they were found, or if they have travelled long distances, perhaps through trade. Similar information can be gained by analysing the metal ores used to make a dagger or sword. Botanists can sometimes find the impressions of grain accidentally buried in the surface of a pot and baked into it when it was fired. This gives us information about early crop production. Atomic physics helps in the dating of museum objects by producing what are called radio-carbon dates (Fig. 3). These give us accurate estimates of age for certain objects stretching back 10,000 years or more before the present. Radio-carbon dating was discovered in America in 1949 by Willard F. Libby. He found that the cosmic rays in the atmosphere form radioactive Carbon 14, which combines with oxygen in the air to make carbon dioxide. This is absorbed by plants and the animals that feed upon them, and in that way passes into all living things. At death, the amount of radioactive carbon in bones or plant charcoal can be measured. Since it was originally estimated that this amount decreases by exactly half every 5,568 years, it is possible to work out how long ago the specimen died. Since 1949 discoveries have shown that there were errors in the system, but these have now been corrected by cross-checking the dates with the oldest tree-rings in the world, those of the Californian bristle-cone pine (*Pinus aristata*), some of which are 4,600 years old.

3 The equipment used for radiocarbon dating in the British Museum Research Laboratory

Archaeologists help prehistorians to write the story of early man. By carefully planned excavations they can piece together the story of the past. We all know that if we leave an old can or brick lying in the hedgerow, grass soon grows over it and it becomes lost. The autumn leaves and weeds soon hide it from view and in a short time it is buried. This process has always happened and helps to explain why ancient objects now lie beneath the ground. Some of course were deliberately buried, but others have been slowly covered through the years by rotting vegetation and the activity of earthworms and burrowing animals. In towns they have been accidentally buried beneath centuries of rubbish. Similarly a building or whole town can slowly fall into ruin, and become choked with weeds until it eventually disappears from view.

It is the archaeologist's job to uncover these objects and buildings. By stripping off the turf and methodically digging down layer by layer, he works backwards through the centuries until he gets down to the earliest ground surface below which there is nothing made by man. The longer ago that an object was dropped, the deeper it is likely to be, with more recent material above it. Imagine placing a penny on a table, with an envelope on top of it

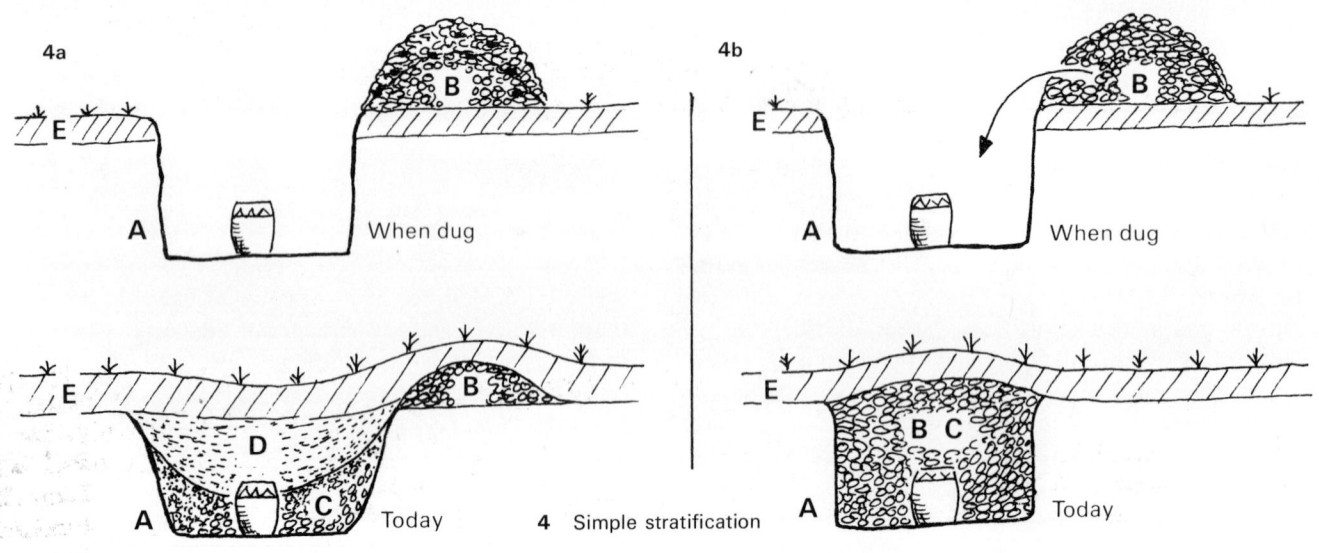

4   Simple stratification

5 This aerial photograph, taken over Long Wittenham in Berkshire, shows a large number of Bronze Age, Iron Age and Roman sites all revealed by 'crop-marks'

and a book above that. It is reasonable for someone looking at the pile to assume that the penny was put down first, since it is below the envelope, and that the book must have been put down last, as it is at the top. Archaeologists call this layering of objects one above the other stratigraphy. It is hardly ever as simple as our coin and book, and it often needs careful thought to decide which layer of soil formed first, or which pit was the first to be cut into it.

Fig. 4a shows a simple example of a small pit (A). When it was dug the material was piled into a heap (B). A pot was placed in the pit, which was not filled in. During the winter, wind and rain and frost caused part of the heap to fall back into the pit (C), covering the pot.

Slowly the sides weathered down and the pit silted up (D) until it was buried beneath the present turf (E).

If the pit had been filled in immediately after the pot had been placed in it (Fig. 4b), the stratigraphy would have been quite different and weathering would have played very little part. It would not have been possible to replace all the soil, some of which would have made a small mound over the top of the pit. Incidentally the looser filling of the pit would probably cause any plants growing over it to grow higher and more strongly, giving a clue to the position of the buried pit. These marks in the crop can easily be spotted from an aeroplane and if photographed from the air can lead archaeologists to unsuspected sites (Fig. 5).

2 · In the Beginning: the Old Stone Age

The first recognizable men in the world probably appeared at least two million years ago. Archaeologists call the period when these first men lived the Old Stone Age or Palaeolithic, and it was during this enormously long stretch of time that the so-called Ice Ages occurred. We now know that there have been at least four Ice Ages, periods of great cold varying immensely in length, with long warm interglacial periods between them. What caused the Ice Ages is not completely understood, but one theory suggests that there were a series of variations in the heat given out by the sun which caused intense changes in the earth's temperature and climate. At its coldest the whole of Ireland, and most of England along a line from Bristol to Oxford and Ipswich, were covered by sheets of ice hundreds of metres thick. In the warmest part of the interglacial periods, some of southern Ireland and west Wales were ice-free, and the line zig-zagged across England to Yorkshire. It is clear that at no time was a great deal of Britain free from ice, and it can scarcely have proved very attractive to early man. Fig. 6 shows the Ice Ages and the warm interglacial periods between them. As you can see, the Great Interglacial period is about four times as long as the others.

Southern England during an Ice Age would have been a bleak and barren place. The ground was treeless and often frozen, with patches of low scrub here and there of the sort known today around the Arctic Circle as tundra. In this countryside roamed herds of reindeer, the woolly rhinoceros, the mammoth with its long, hairy coat and curving tusks, the cave bear and the bison. The interglacial times brought much warmer, almost tropical conditions. The melting ice created great rivers and lakes with thick lush vegetation to shelter the straight-tusked elephant, the two-horned rhinoceros, the hippopotamus and sabre-toothed tiger, as well as less ferocious bison, deer, wild cattle and horses.

About 500,000 years ago the first men appeared in Britain. Where the earliest men had originated we are not sure, but probably in central Africa or north-west India. Now they wandered into southern Britain as hunters following the animals and birds, and temporarily camping beside the rivers and streams. At that time England was still joined to the continent of Europe. Very few traces of these people have survived today, except for

6 The approximate length of the Ice Ages

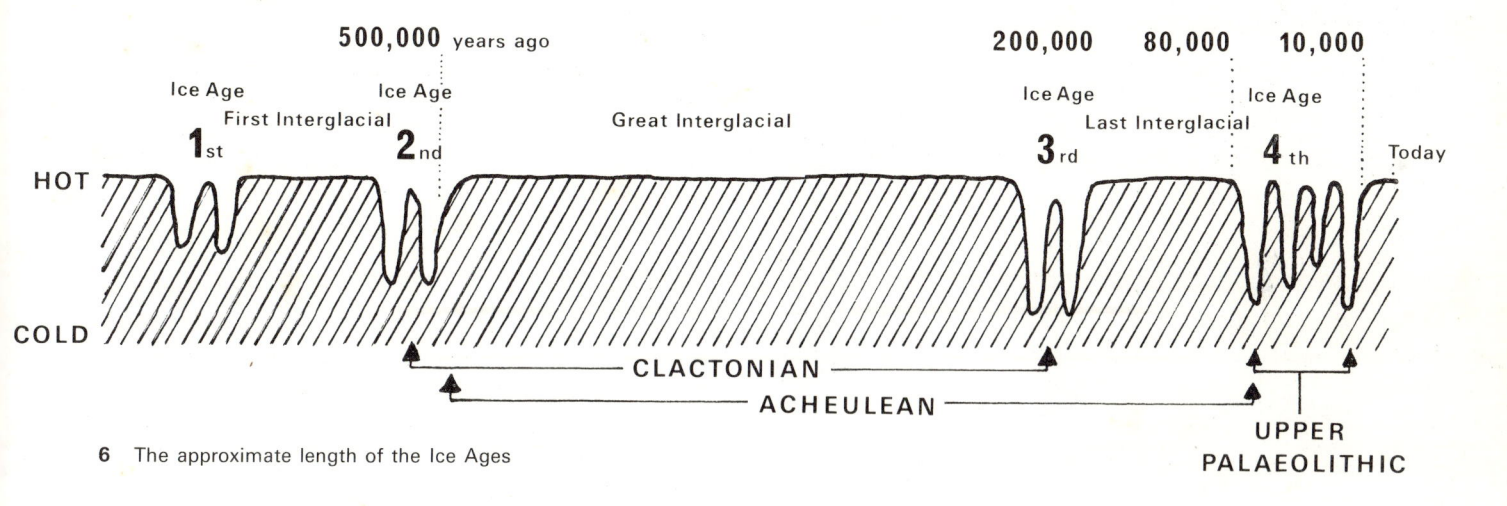

the tools of flint and stone which they fashioned. Sometimes the places where these implements were made can be found buried under clay and gravel in quarries in the south of England. In western England and France the rock shelters and cave mouths in which men spent the long winter months contain layers of their rubbish which accumulated over thousands of years.

Archaeologists call the first part of the Old Stone Age until the end of the last interglacial period, the Lower Palaeolithic, whilst men living during the last Ice Age belong to the Upper Palaeolithic.

The earliest human remains found in Britain belonging to the Lower Palaeolithic were pieces of a skull found in the Lower Thames at Swanscombe in Kent. It dates from the Great Interglacial period and was found with tools of the Acheulean type which are described below. The skull is incomplete but it seems to belong to a man of early *Homo sapiens* type, the group to which we ourselves belong. Anthropologists, who study primitive people, are still very uncertain about the earliest true men. There seem to have been two kinds of early people, *homo sapiens* and *homo sapiens neanderthalensis*. The second group,

7 An Acheulean hand-axe being used to remove bark from a tree, in search of grubs and insects for food

neanderthalensis (named after a skull found at Neanderthal in Germany) sheltered in caves and practised careful burial ceremonies, but died out for reasons that we do not understand. It is *homo sapiens* (wise man) who survived and formed our direct ancestors.

When we visit a museum we can often see cases filled with stone tools of early man. They suggest that he made hundreds of them at a time, but you must remember that they were in fact made over thousands of years, although a number of them might have been made by one man in a single day. We should also remember that early man made many other tools of wood and bone which have not survived for us to find. Some archaeologists have suggested that the population of Britain in the Lower Palaeolithic period was probably little more than a hundred people.

Tools were made by taking a block of flint or hard stone and chipping from it sharp-edged cutting implements, some of which are called 'hand-axes', although we have to admit that we are uncertain of all their uses, which probably included cutting and skinning animals, as well as grubbing-up edible roots and insects (Fig. 7). When a block of flint was struck with a large pebble or bone, a series of flakes were detached. These flakes might be trimmed and made into cutting blades and knives, or they might be discarded and the core of the flint used instead as a 'hand-axe' of either pear or oval shape. In England the earliest tools so far recognized were of the flake type and are called Clactonian after the seaside town of Clacton, where some of them were found. The hand axes were made later. They were pear-shaped at first, and then oval. They belong to a type which stayed much the same for thousands of years and are called Acheulean (after the town of St Acheul in France). The fact that the Acheulean tools remained the same for so long suggests

8 Acheulean hand-axes

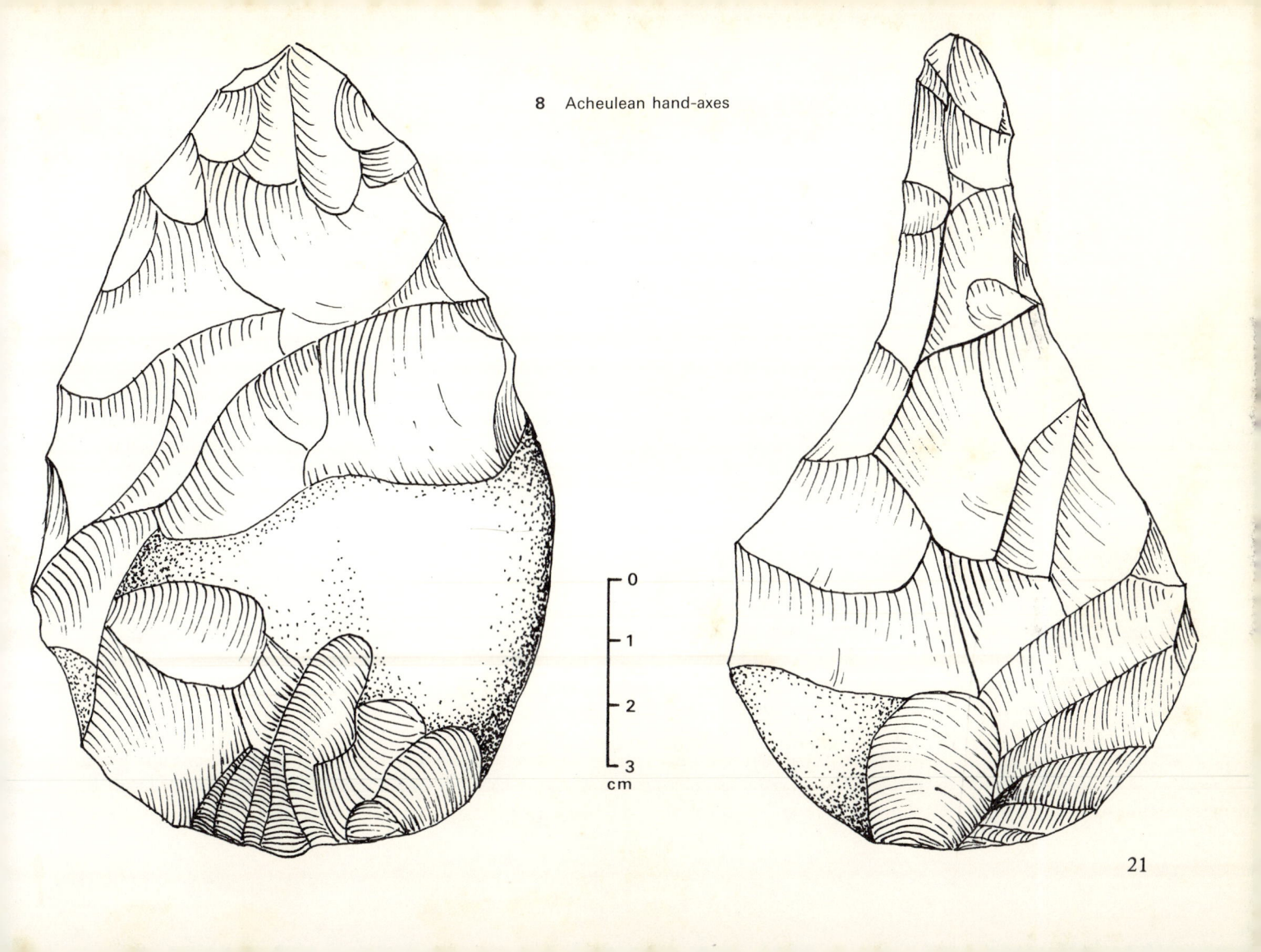

that man's way of life changed very little and that his powers of invention had scarcely developed (Fig. 8).

The flint implements can tell us very little about the everyday life of their makers. There is little doubt that they moved about, following the animals that provided them with food, or camping beside streams and lakes where they could fish and snare birds that came to the water's edge. They probably used fishing lines and nets, as well as baskets, for trapping. They also ate nuts, berries, edible roots and fungi. They sometimes made simple shelters for themselves with branches or animal hides, draping them over a bush or rough timber framework to form a tent. Or they sheltered under overhanging rocks, as at Oldbury in Kent and High Rocks in Sussex. If there was a cave nearby, they might establish a home for the winter in its mouth, though they did not live deep underground, where they would have needed constant artificial light and heat, and would soon have developed rheumatism owing to the dampness of the caves. Fire was one of man's first discoveries. He probably learned how to make it from the sparks that were given off when he chipped flint. With it he had heat, light and protection from the wild animals who also lived in the caves. The remains of these Palaeolithic men and their tools and weapons have been found at Wookey Hole and Gough's Cave in Cheddar. Hyaenas had also lived in the cave at Wookey and the excavators discovered the gnawed bones of hundreds of animals. These included four hundred wild horses, two hundred woolly rhinoceros and many bison, cave bear, reindeer, elk and mammoth. From this list it is clear that there were plenty of animals for man to hunt.

A wooden spear-tip from Clacton and numerous bone harpoons give us a clue as to how men caught their food, but there is no certainty that they invented the bow and arrow. They probably used deadfall traps in which heavy logs fell on their victims, or dug pits to trap the larger beasts. Sometimes they drove them over high cliffs, where they fell to their deaths.

From the skeletons of men living in Britain during the last Ice Age, it is clear that they looked very much like us; they were generally tall and fairly slender in build. Of course we cannot tell the colour of their skin or hair, but it has been suggested after studying the shape of their bones that they were not unlike the North American Indians. None of the skeletons found were of very old people, and probably most of them died very young by our standards — before they were twenty-five. They probably made their clothes from animal skins and sewed them together with bone needles threaded with sinews. Occasionally they wore bangles and beads made from mammoth ivory as decorations.

In Upper Palaeolithic times these early hunters may have tried to use magic to help them catch their prey. Deep in some of the French caves pictures of animals were painted or engraved on the walls. Sometimes these have spears painted across them. The artist or witch-doctor who made the picture may have believed that he would have power over the animal he portrayed, and could kill it at will, or control it, and even take over the strength and skill of the beast itself; this is called sympathetic magic. No paintings have been found in British caves, although a few pieces of engraved bone are known.

Each group of people may have included a witch-doctor, who performed spells as cures for illness, and foretold the future, as happens with primitive peoples in some parts of the world today. Some boys would be apprenticed to the witch-doctor and trained in the mysteries of their tribe. In French caves the footprints of Stone Age boys have been found preserved in the wet clay of the floor; these were probably made by the boys as they performed magic hunting dances and underwent initiation ceremonies which eventually enabled them to become full huntsmen in their tribe. Similar customs are still performed by the Aborigines of Australia, and Bushmen of South Africa.

In the Paviland cave in the Gower peninsula of South Wales the burial of a young man was found in a grave dug into the cave floor. Around it were thick traces of red ochre, a paint that seems to have been spread over the pale corpse to give it the appearance of healthy living flesh. With him were buried some shell beads, and a bangle of mammoth ivory, whilst nearby was the skull of a mammoth that may have been intended as a food offering. This is the first evidence from Britain that men thought it necessary to bury the dead. The objects buried with the corpse were probably intended for his use in the next world and suggest that these people believed in a life after death.

At the close of the last Ice Age there were people living in a number of cave sites in Britain from Derbyshire to South Wales and Somerset. They left many small flake tools, knife blades and harpoons which must have been used for hunting as well as bone needles, which would have been used for sewing skins together to make clothes. These late Upper Palaeolithic people are known as Creswellian after caves at Creswell Crags in Derbyshire. Their tools and weapons have also been found in caves in the Mendips and in the Gower peninsula, and at Kent's Cavern, Torquay.

3 · Britain Becomes an Island: the Middle Stone Age

10,000 to 4000 BC

The end of the last Ice Age was a very slow affair, spread over many centuries. For people living at the time it would not have seemed noticeably warmer, but very slowly, as the ice melted and retreated northwards, the arctic tundra vegetation of Britain was replaced by the first scattered birch, pine and willow trees. The herds of reindeer and wild horses preferred to move northwards with the ice, but for man the environment began to change for the better. There were still plenty of lakes and rivers but lush grasses and shrubs now grew amongst the trees, and gradually as it became warmer and moister hazel, oak, elm, lime and alder trees covered the land. Their pollen was blown into peat bogs, and peat preserves almost anything which falls into it. So palaeo-botanists (scientists who study plants of ancient times) can now observe this pollen under microscopes and discover something about the early forests and the climate in which they grew.

When Britain was still joined to the Continent, the river Thames flowed eastwards until it joined the river Rhine, and both then ran into the North Sea. With the melting of the Ice Age glaciers an enormous amount of water was released. This caused the sea level to rise and flood the ancient Thames-Rhine estuary. By about 6000 BC the English Channel had formed, though at first it was little more than a wide, marshy river, and could be fairly easily crossed.

As we have said, many of the larger animals that Palaeolithic man had hunted moved northwards away from Britain. Others had become extinct. Clearly man now had to adapt himself to changing conditions. He had to eat more of the abundant berries and plants, and hunt the smaller animals in the woods and marshes. They included elk, wild cattle, roe deer, the brown bear and the wild boar, as well as fish and birds. Although the thick forests made movement more difficult, he cut down trees with a specially designed axe, and used the wood for making shelters, boats, spears, bows and a host of other things, as well as for firewood. This period of change, following the last Ice Age, is known as the Middle Stone Age or Mesolithic.

When it began, around 10,000 BC, Britain and the continent were still joined together and we know of one group of people who wandered between Scandinavia and eastern England. These people are sometimes known as Maglemosians after the Magle Mosse (or fen) where their remains were first studied in Denmark. They are most easily identified by the long rectangular flint axes that they made, together with minute flint blades called microliths which were probably mounted with resin into bone and wooden handles, whilst others were used as heads for wooden bows and arrows. They carved bones and antlers to make barbed harpoons and spears which they used for fishing and hunting. They shaped fish-hooks from bone, and wove willow twigs into fish-traps (often with birch-bark floats), and baskets. Objects of Maglemosian type have been found extensively in Denmark and eastern England, and even dredged from the North Sea (Fig. 9).

At Star Carr in east Yorkshire, not far from Scarborough, excavators found a crude birch wood platform beside a lake on which Mesolithic folk may have lived during the summer months. Many perishable objects had been preserved because the site was waterlogged and the air was kept away from them. The excavators could see the marks of the stone axes on the trees used to make the platform. They found rolls of birch-bark, which had probably been used to provide birch-pitch, with which arrowheads and microliths could be glued to wooden shafts. Picks made of elk antler may have been used in digging out edible roots. Many bone harpoons survived, and numerous specimens of bracket fungus, which were perhaps gathered by the Mesolithic women as tinder for their fires. Bones of red deer, elk, wild pig and roe deer,

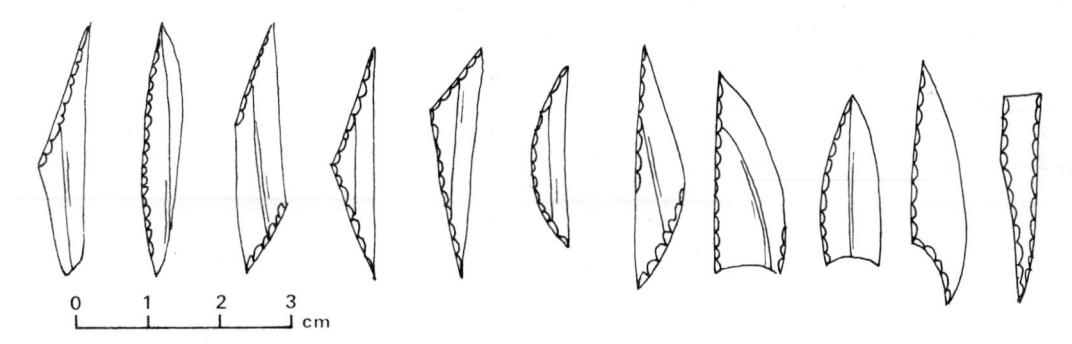

9 Typical microliths (after Professor Clark)

as well as water-fowl, showed what animals and birds had been caught. If the Star Carr people fished then the bones of the fish have not been preserved. An unexpected find was deer antlers still attached to parts of the animals' skulls. They had been perforated in such a way that they could be worn as masks and perhaps they were used for decoying deer or for some ceremonial purpose of the type recalled by the horn-dance which is still performed each year at Abbot's Bromley in Staffordshire. A wooden paddle indicated that the Star Carr people had travelled on the lake, though no traces of their boats were found Canoes made from hollowed-out tree-trunks have been found elsewhere in Britain, and some may belong to the Mesolithic period.

Other Mesolithic people chose to live on the sand and gravel ridges of Britain, where the ground was drier and the woodland not so thick. They have left little trace of themselves for archaeologists to find, except for their tiny flint tools, which must have been stuck with resin into wooden shafts as spears or arrows. We do know that these people made tent-like summer shelters out of wood and skins, and traces of these have been found in the Isle of Man and the Pennines. A hut site was found at Abinger Common in Surrey in 1950 and it can still be visited. It consisted of an oval pit measuring 4.3 metres by 3 metres, and 1 metre deep, with traces of fire at one end. Around it ran a gravel bench, and two holes for posts probably supported a lean-to roof. More than a thousand micro-lithic flints were found on the floor. Whether the hut had been used for working or sleeping is uncertain, though it would have been very cramped for either.

The people of the gravel lands had dogs to help them in their hunting. Their skeletons suggest that they were probably descended from wolves that their predecessors learnt to domesticate.

In the islands off western Scotland and north-west Ireland mounds of sea shells, called middens, represent the discarded rubbish of another Mesolithic group called Obanians (from Oban in Scotland). These people seem to have lived mainly on fish and shell-fish, together with red deer and wild pig, and to have trapped sea birds like gulls and cormorants and even the now extinct great auk. They used bone and antler harpoons with double barbs as weapons to catch their prey. Vast quantities of shells were piled on to the middens, making some of them many feet thick. In one of them a large shelter was dug with a roof supported on six posts. This eventually became buried as more rubbish was piled on top of it.

4 · The First Farmers: the Early Neolithic

4000 to 3500 BC

The British Isles were well-wooded and well-watered by the time that small groups of farmers from Europe began to move in, about 4000 BC. Farming and the domestication of animals had both begun in Palestine or Kurdistan (in Turkey) about 10,000 years ago, and they revolutionized the life of early man. The people there had discovered that the seeds of wild wheat, barley and millet were good to eat, and that by planting these seeds they could make the crop grow almost anywhere they liked. They may have accidentally dropped wild seeds, and then noticed that new plants grew where the seed had fallen. This meant that instead of travelling long distances in seach of the wild grasses, they could grow them conveniently beside their homes. Similarly, they learnt to tame the wild cattle, sheep and goats and kept them in pens where they could milk them, eat them and use their skins for clothing. Now that they no longer depended on hunting for their food, they began to live in one place. They established permanent villages, and from some of these, later on, grew the first towns.

Even so, man did move slowly across Europe. A settled life had probably led to bigger families and the need for more land. As the farmers moved, their neighbours copied their ideas, and perhaps gave them new ones in exchange. The arrival of these farming folk marks the beginning of the New Stone Age or Neolithic period, which is divided into three parts: the Early Neolithic (4000 to 3500 BC) when the farmers were settling in and adjusting themselves to British conditions; the Middle Neolithic (3500 to 2500 BC), which has left most evidence of their religious and ceremonial beliefs; and the Late Neolithic (2500 to 2100 BC), when new immigrant Beaker people appear in Britain and soon dominate the scene.

After a series of prospecting expeditions in which the farmers landed at various points along the coasts of Britain, they eventually made their way along river valleys on to the gravels and chalk hills of southern England, which, although wooded, drained easily and lacked the thick undergrowth of the clay lands. Such land was easy to till and often provided openings for pasture where sheep and goats, and cattle and pigs could graze. The farmers had to make additional clearings in the woods, and they used stone axes that had been care-

10 A reconstructed polished-stone axe. A polished Neolithic axe-head with a modern handle, copied from an original example, in Moesgaard Museum, near Aarhus, Denmark

11 Polished-stone axes in use. Axes like the one shown above are being used to chop down a tree. It took about eight minutes

fully polished to give them sharp cutting edges (Figs. 10 and 11). Once they had felled the trees, and laid aside the straightest branches for building, they burned the rest and hoed the ash into the ground, which they then planted with seed. Later they harvested the crop, using flint sickle blades mounted in wooden handles. Although the soil soon became exhausted and had to be abandoned, grazing animals prevented the trees from growing again, and so large areas of open downland slowly appeared. The farmers may have built rectangular one-roomed huts near the plots. Few have been found, but this may be due to the perishable nature of the wood from which they were made. There would have been many tracks through the woods, linking settlements, but the main routeways would have followed recognizable landmarks like streams and the edge of the hills.

The chalk and limestone hills of southern England are arranged like the spokes of a wheel, branching out from the hub, which is Salisbury Plain (Fig. 12). Along these hills ran the main prehistoric routeways, which still exist. They have names like Ridgeway, Icknield Way and Pilgrim's Way – names which are many centuries old, but

12 The ridgeways of southern Britain. The dots represent forests; the horizontal dashes show fenland

not nearly as old as the tracks themselves. Perhaps there is a ridgeway near your home. In the stone country of the north and west, similar tracks ran across the moors. Their routes were often marked by large cairns (piles of stones), and they linked the places where Early Neolithic men lived.

In the first 500 years of the Neolithic period the farmers spread quickly over most of Britain, and whilst the hills of the south may have seemed attractive, we know that they also settled beside marshes and lakes in north-western England and in Ireland. Unfortunately wooden houses leave little trace, and all too often archaeologists find stone tools, bones and sometimes pottery, but no obvious indication of where the farm stood. Some of these remains are scattered over fairly wide areas, suggesting that small villages may have existed.

In order to fell trees Neolithic man needed axes, and he soon discovered that the best stone for these does not come from the ground surface, where it is likely to have been fractured by the frost, but from deep underground. Because of this he dug mines for flint and quarries for stone (Fig. 14).

Flint, almost pure silica, 'grows' or forms in layers in the chalk, which may lie deep in the ground or outcrop at the surface. The earliest flint mines that have been excavated are at Cissbury and Harrow Hill in Sussex (Fig. 13), but the best known group is that in Norfolk at Grimes Graves, where the mines spread over more than thirty acres, and about 360 mine shafts and almost as many pits lie buried under modern sand and grass. When the flint outcropped near the surface, it was worked by the open-cast method, which meant simply digging it straight from the ground in quarries. Where the seam was only 2 or 3 metres down, vertical shafts were sunk side by side, and the flint nodules removed from the area uncovered at the bottom. But when the seams of flint became really deep, 6 metres or more, then a single shaft was sunk from the surface, and low tunnels radiated out from the bottom to follow the stone for 9 to 12 metres. Rough pillars of undug chalk were left between the tunnels, which became veritable rabbit warrens. The chalk removed from a shaft was filled-back into an exhausted one. Sometimes new tunnels accidentally ran into the old shafts and then there might be a fall of loose rubble that could sometimes prove fatal.

The miners dug the flint from the pits by using deer antler picks and bone wedges which were hammered into the surrounding chalk, and then levered out, loosening the flint as they came. The nodules were then scraped with shoulder blades of oxen or deer into baskets and hauled by ropes to the surface of the shaft, where the final implements were made. Where there were underground galleries in the mines they were lit by small lamps, hollowed from chalk, burning animal fat and moss wicks.

13   Inside a flint mine on Harrow Hill in Sussex at the time of its excavation in 1925

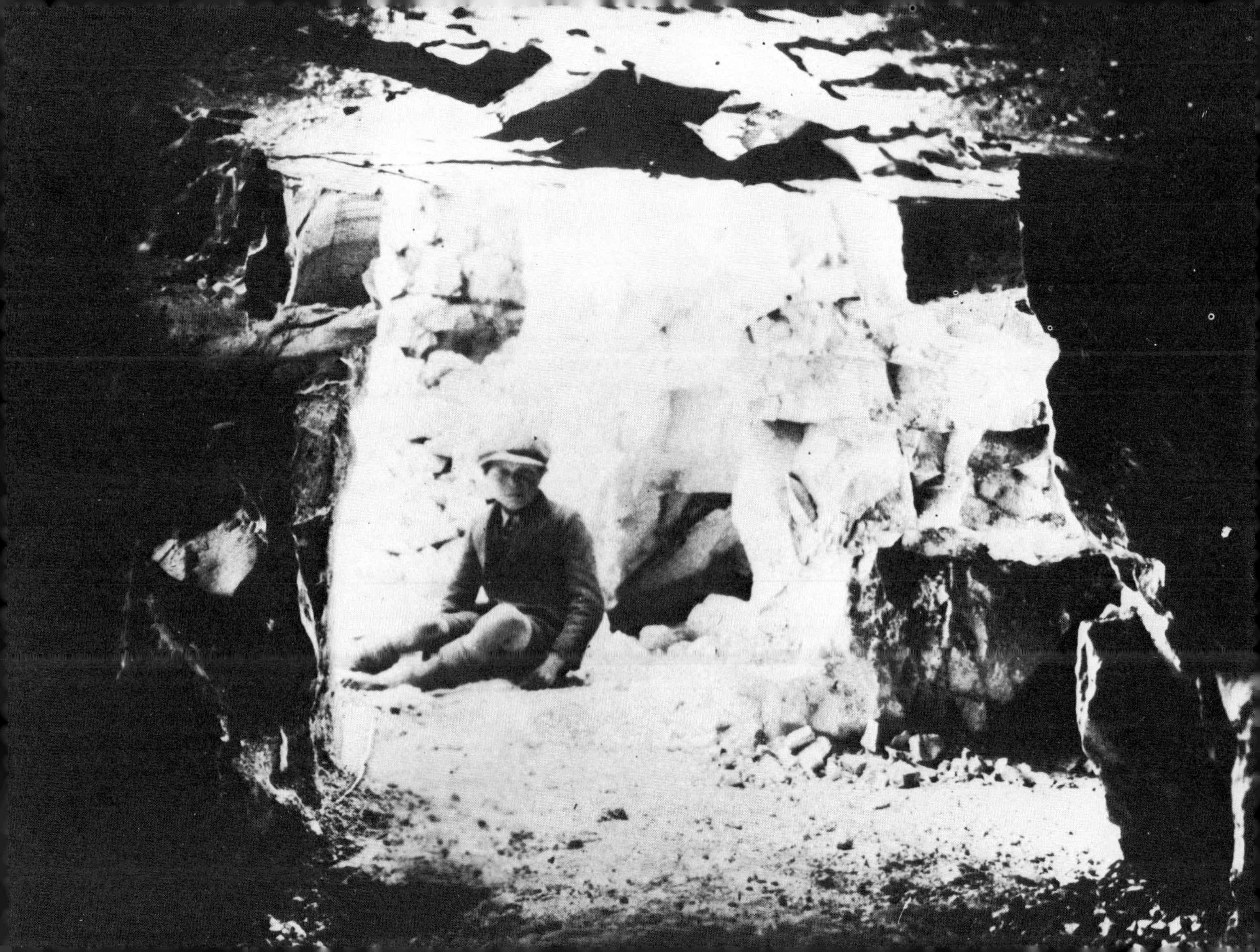

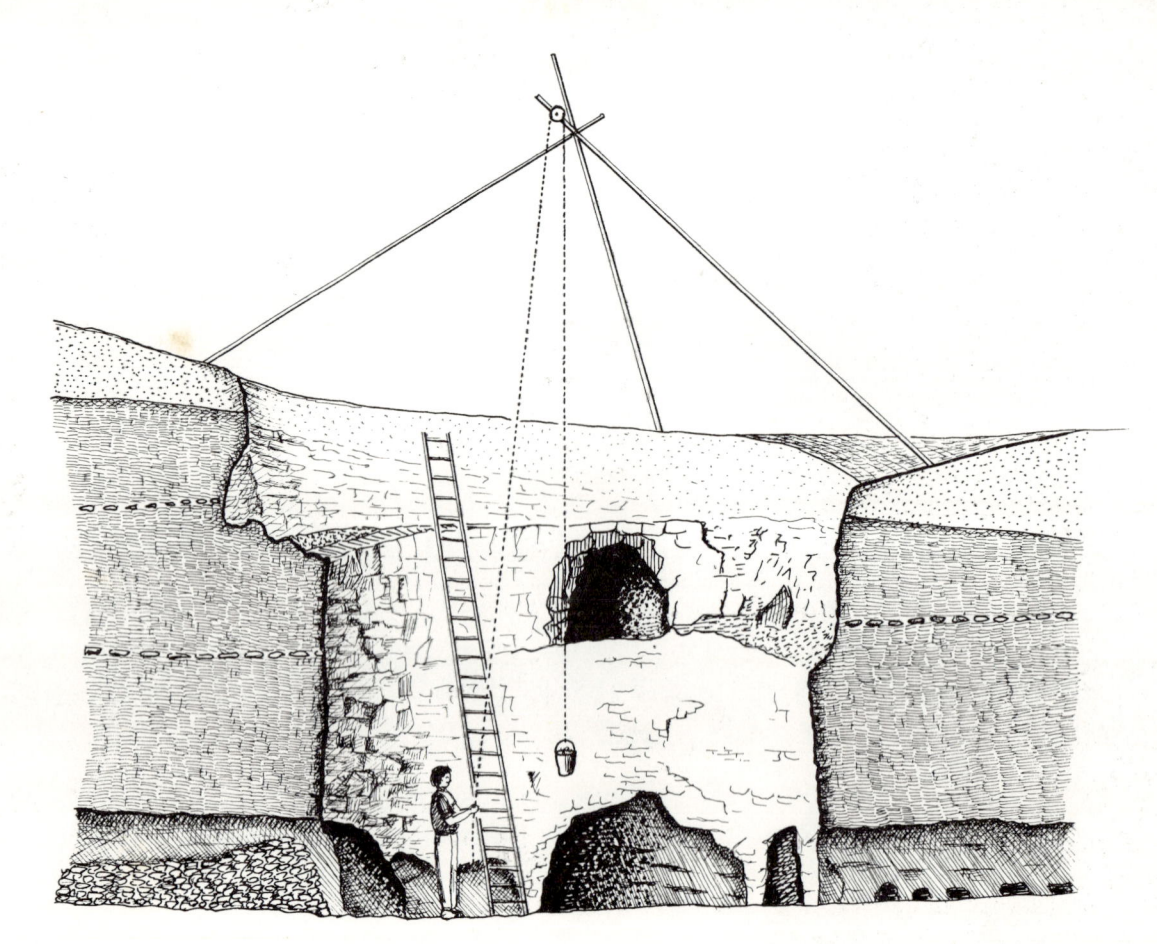

14 A section of one of the Harrow Hill flint mines (after Robert Gurd)

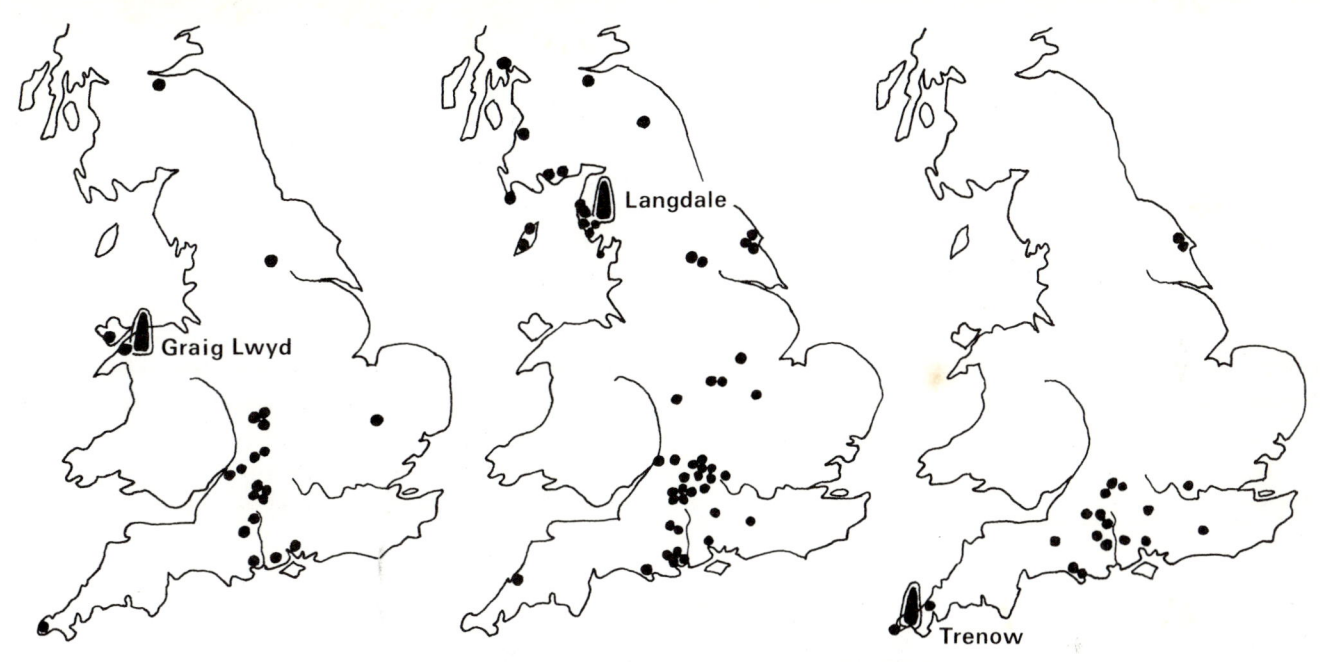

15 Three British stone axe factories. The dots show where the axes have been found. (After J. F. Stone)

We know that there must have been some form of trade in these axes, because they are found in various parts of the country. But we are not sure if some of the miners carried the implements all over Britain for exchange, or if Neolithic tribesmen came to the mines, or indeed if there was a third group of 'middlemen' who collected the axes and peddled them along the ridgeways. There would be little digging during the winter when the ground was frozen, but during the summer the flint diggers would be so busy mining that they would have little time to grow or catch their own food. So they were the first industrial workers to depend on exchanging their products for food and clothing. The flint mines of Norfolk have been dated by radio-carbon to between 3000 and 2500 BC whilst those of Sussex are considerably earlier, and were dug about 3750 BC.

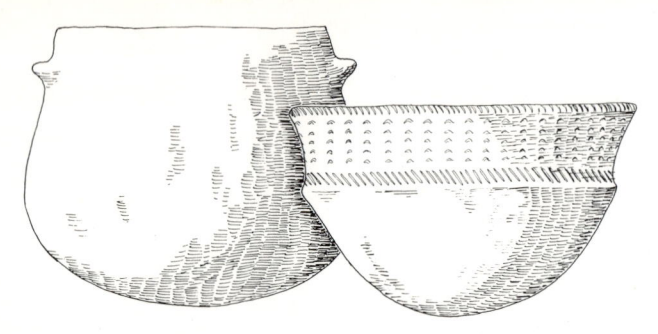

16 Early Neolithic pottery (after Stuart Piggott)

17 An Early Neolithic bowl (*left*) from the West Kennet long barrow, and a Late Neolithic pot with twisted-cord decoration, from Wilsford (both in Wiltshire)

In the areas of western Britain, where there is no flint, but where suitable stone outcropped, axes were made of such igneous rocks as greenstone from around Trenowin in Cornwall and volcanic tuff from the Langdale in the Lake District. Other stone came from Craig Lwyd in north Wales and Tievebulliagh in Ulster. Axes from all these 'factories' were traded extensively in Britain, as can be seen from the maps which show places where they have been found (Fig. 15). In order to break the very hard stone, lumps of it were first heated to a high temperature over a fire, and then suddenly cooled by pouring cold water over them. This caused the stone to contract rapidly and shatter, breaking into many pieces, some of which could then be chipped into axe-heads.

The early Neolithic farmers were the first people in Britain to make pottery (Fig. 16). Sometimes they coiled long sausages of clay into the shapes of the vessels, which they may have fired in dome-shaped kilns close to their homes. In the beginning they copied leather containers and produced round-bottomed baggy-shaped pots, often with small protruding ear-like handles or lugs. Occasionally they imitated the stitching on the original leather vessels by adding simple decorations to the pots. Later their pottery became much more ornate, and they often made patterns by pressing small bones or their finger-tips into the wet clay. Some of the Middle and Late Neolithic pots seem to imitate baskets (Fig. 17).

5 · Religion and Burials: the Middle Neolithic
3500 to 2500 BC

On the chalk hills and in a few river valleys along the routeways of southern England the farmers of the Middle Neolithic period constructed a series of roughly circular enclosures. These consist of a single, or two to four concentric rings of ditches interrupted by many causeways of undug chalk. The material from the ditches has been piled up into low internal banks, and they enclose anything up to twenty acres of land.

When first discovered, these sites were thought to be the camps in which Neolithic man lived, and they were called 'causewayed camps'. We now know that they were not permanently occupied and it is more difficult to explain them. Although small pits and post-holes have been found in some of these 'camps' they do not add up to any clear pattern that tells us how they were used. What is more intriguing is that deposits of rubbish, perhaps scraped from the floors of huts or settlements elsewhere, were deliberately placed in the ditches and covered with soil from the banks. This seems very curious to us and difficult to understand. The rubbish buried, which includes pieces of pottery and animal bone, may have been connected with some recently dead person, and perhaps burying it was thought to have some magical effect that would enable the person to live again. This does not explain the curious causeways through the ditches, unless they were pathways for the spirit of the dead person.

Perhaps the 'camps' were used as tribal meeting places where scattered groups of people, the local farmers and the wandering traders, came together to make laws, to celebrate certain feasts and to perform religious ceremonies connected with the well-being of the tribe, such as initiations, marriages and burials. More than eighteen of these 'causewayed camps' have now been discovered in England. The best known is at Windmill Hill in Wiltshire, and its name is often given to the Neolithic farmers in southern England, who are loosely called the Windmill Hill folk.

Towards the end of the Middle Neolithic period people began to construct roughly circular banked enclosures with ditches on the inside that we now call 'henges' or henge monuments. These, too, seem to have been connected with ceremonies of a religious nature. Some people consider that as time went by henge monuments

35

18 The henge monument of Avebury in Wiltshire

replaced causewayed camps. Some henges have a single entrance, others have two opposite each other, and Avebury seems to have four. All of them have a bank of earth or stones which is separated from a flat central area or platform by a ditch. Onlookers may have sat or stood on the bank and looked across the ditch at the ceremonies taking place inside. We tend to think that these were of a religious nature, but perhaps law-making, trials or even sporting events, could have taken place there.

Some henge monuments that have been excavated contained holes for posts. These might have been free-standing like Indian totem poles, or have supported wooden buildings. Occasionally there are burials within the henge. The monuments are usually situated close to water, and sometimes on sloping ground. They vary in size from as little as 9 metres in diameter to as much as 490 metres. There are good examples at King Arthur's Round Table near Penrith and Thornborough near Ripon in the north, and in the south at Avebury and Stonehenge, though both of these probably belong to the Late Neolithic period and Stonehenge has been altered a number of times (Fig. 18).

The elaborate burial methods of the Middle Neolithic people help us to know a little more about their attitude to death. It was normal for a number of people to be buried in the same tomb. Since they didn't all die at once the tomb had to be one that could be opened to take new burials on a number of occasions, or else the corpses had to be stored in some temporary place until enough had accumulated for a mass burial.

In south-eastern Britain, in what archaeologists refer to as the lowland zone (where no hills are higher than 1,000 feet [304 metres]), bodies were placed in wooden mortuary huts where they were kept for some time, often slowly decaying, till only the bones remained and enough had accumulated to warrant building a tomb for them. Sometimes this was for as many as fifty corpses. Members of the tribe making the burial probably came together for ceremonies that may have lasted many weeks. The most important event would be the piling of a large mound of earth, often 60 or 90 metres long, over the mortuary hut until it was completely buried. The soil was obtained by digging two deep and roughly parallel ditches along either side of it and thus creating an earthen long barrow. Sometimes a special new enclosure of wood or turf was constructed to hold the corpses or bones before the mound was built over them. At all events, once buried these timber burial chambers could not be re-entered, and after a few years the timbers would have rotted and probably collapsed.

In Dorset a small series of remarkably long earthen barrows have been found and are called bank-barrows. There are good examples on Martin's Down (Long Bredy) and at Came Wood in Broadmayne parish. The best-known example stretches the length of Maiden Castle,

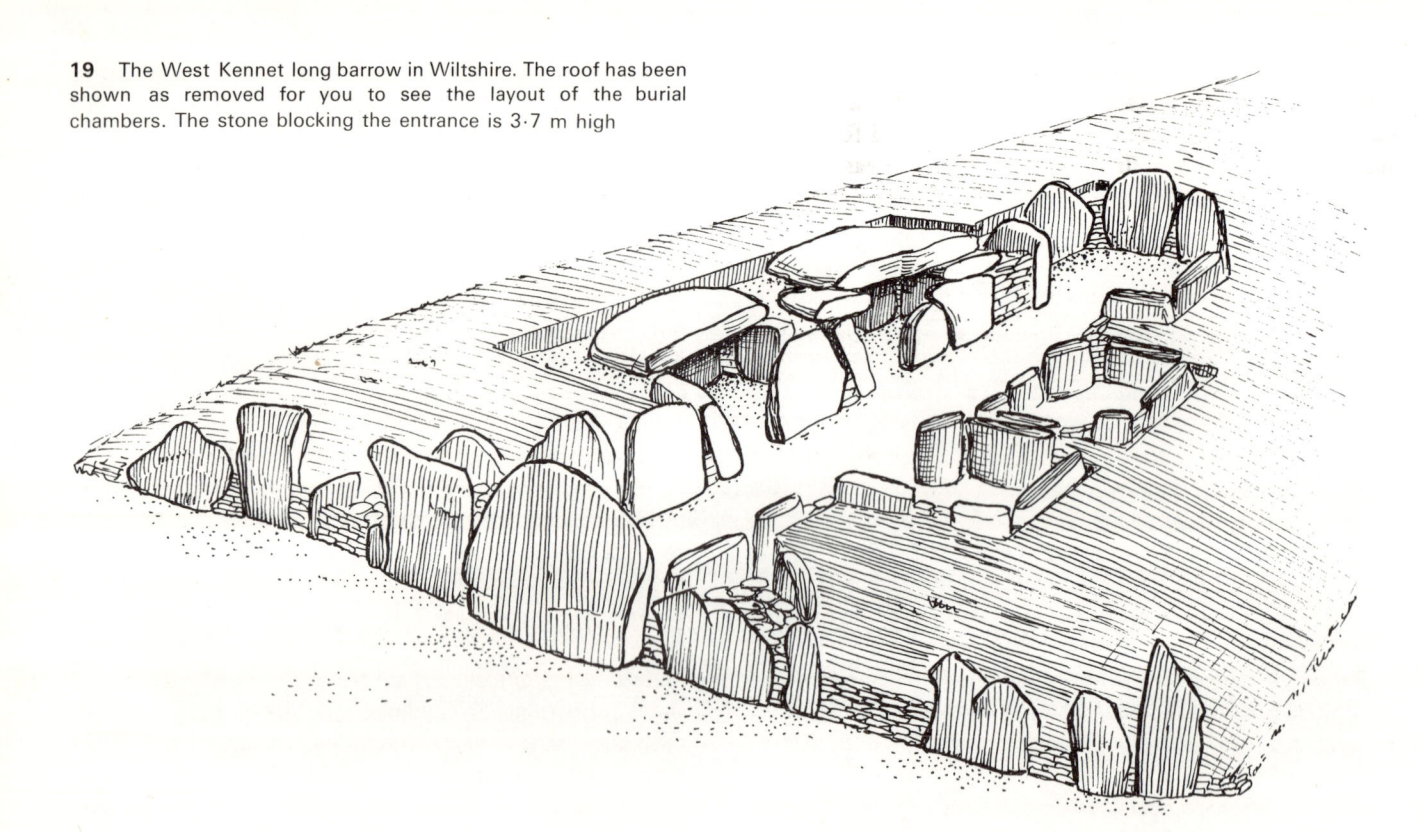

19 The West Kennet long barrow in Wiltshire. The roof has been shown as removed for you to see the layout of the burial chambers. The stone blocking the entrance is 3·7 m high but it is very difficult to see as it is now only a few centimetres high, owing to ploughing.

Some of the long barrows are connected with long parallel-sided ditched enclosures called cursuses. Yet again, we have little idea of their purpose, but imagine that they were used in funeral ceremonies; perhaps, as Stukeley suggested 200 years ago, for funeral games, races and processions. One, nearly 2.8 kilometres long, lies north of Stonehenge. The longest of all, the Dorset cursus, is more than 9.6 kilometres (6 miles) long and only 82 metres wide. It is best seen where it is cut by the road from Cranborne to Sixpenny Handley.

Earthen long barrows can be found on the chalk hills of southern England, Lincolnshire and east Yorkshire, with a small number in East Anglia. In some of the Yorkshire long barrows the bodies of the dead were cremated; this doesn't seem to have happened in other areas, although a few bodies in the southern barrows show signs of partial burning. The Yorkshire long-barrow builders made pottery bowls with wide mouths; similar bowls are also found in the Scottish Lowlands, Ulster and the Isle of Man.

In western England and Wales, where there is an abundance of stone suitable for building, the long barrows were constructed with stone burial chambers. They are sometimes known as the Severn-Cotswold tombs. They consisted of long galleries, often with two or three pairs of side chambers, buried under a long mound

20 Inside the West Kennet long barrow. The boys are standing in the circular chamber at the end of the 12-metres-long gallery

39

21 Wayland's Smithy is an easily accessible gallery grave beside the Ridgeway in north Berkshire

of earth and stones (Figs 19–21). The gallery could be entered from one end of the barrow, though it would normally be sealed with a large blocking stone that would only be moved when a burial was to take place. Because the stone chambers, unlike wooden ones, would not rot, the tomb could be used again and again for hundreds of years until it was full. Whenever a new burial was put into the tomb, the bones of the earlier corpses were moved to the back of the chambers and stacked in neat piles of leg bones and skulls and so on. Perhaps this was a job for some old person in the community, as it is today in some Swiss and Austrian mountain villages where land is scarce.

Some of the Severn-Cotswold tombs have dummy or false entrances at their higher ends and the true burial chambers are hidden in the sides of the mound. This might have been done to fool tomb robbers. Belas Knap and Rodmarton in the Cotswolds are examples of this type of tomb. In the Clyde estuary and northern Ireland a related form of gallery grave was constructed in which the long gallery was divided into compartments along its length by stone slabs or sills, and burials were made in each of the sections in turn. These tombs were often situated close to the settlements of the folk who built them.

Since some of the tombs remained in use for hundreds of years, we may assume that religious beliefs changed very little. We might compare them with burial in a Christian cathedral or parish church that has been in use for hundreds of years. There have been changes in the church ritual but the idea of Christianity has remained unchanged. Pieces of pottery and animal bones (representing joints of meat) have been found in front of the blocking stone at the mouth of the tombs, and sometimes in the material of the barrow mound itself, so it is clear that funeral feasts and offerings to the dead were made at intervals. Perhaps the pots contained food or drink, and were ceremonially smashed during the feast.

Along the western coasts of Britain can be found another form of burial place, the passage grave. This consisted of a roughly circular burial chamber, approached by a long passage from the entrance, and the whole enclosed within a circular mound. The main concentration of these tombs is in Ireland in the Boyne valley north of Dublin, but they stretch across central Ireland to the west coast, and are also found in Anglesey and the Scottish islands. A smaller, related form, known as an entrance-grave, can be seen in the Isles of Scilly and south-western Cornwall. Many of the walls of the passage graves are decorated with elaborate patterns of zig-zags, lozenges, spirals and concentric circles 'pecked' into the flat surface of the stones with a flint chisel. Sometimes the decorated stones have no obvious purpose, but stand in front of the drystone walls that support the roof, or are decorated on their buried rear faces. The most magnificent passage grave is at New Grange in Ireland. The passage is 19 metres long and the burial chamber is 5 metres from front to back with three side recesses opening out of it. Near New Grange, at Dowth and Nowth, there are two other passage graves with accessible chambers. In Anglesey, Barclodiad y Gawres contains decorated stones, and another occurs at the passage grave of Bryn Celli Ddu (Fig. 22).

The burials of the Neolithic period are also useful for telling us something about the people themselves. The average height for a man at that time was about 1.63 metres; women were slightly shorter, about 1.55 metres. Few people lived to be older than forty years of age, and many must have died in childhood. The bones show that Neolithic people often adopted a squatting position, and that many suffered from arthritis. There are no signs of complaints such as rickets and scurvy, probably because prehistoric man normally ate plenty of animal fat and fresh green foods.

22 The entrance to the passage grave of Bryn Celli Ddu in Anglesey

6 · The Beaker Folk: the Late Neolithic

2500 to 2100 BC

We know almost nothing about the houses of the Neolithic farmers in Britain, and so we have to turn to Europe to see what they might have been like. The earliest Neolithic houses were of wood, rectangular in shape and sometimes as much as 35 metres long and 5 to 7 metres wide. A village excavated at Köln Lindenthal near Cologne contained more than twenty 'long houses' with walls made of split logs and wattle work daubed with clay. The floors, also of wood, seem to have been raised above ground level on rows of stilts. Many of the houses were divided into two rooms, one no doubt for the family, the other perhaps for storing seed grain. Two even larger 'long houses' were excavated at Barkaer in Denmark and had been built of wattle and daub. One was about 80 metres long and had been divided into twenty-six rooms.

Later, in the Middle Neolithic, smaller, two-roomed houses measuring about 10 metres by 5 metres were built. At Aichbühl in Bavaria twenty-two of these were set up on timber piles beside a lake. Each had an inner and outer room covered by a gabled roof. The outer door was in the end wall of the house. On entering you would see on your right a clay hearth and domed oven. Hot ashes from the hearth were placed in the oven and would heat it sufficiently to bake bread inside it.

The Late Neolithic houses in Europe seem to have been even smaller, about 4.5 metres square, with a single room, some of which contained a hearth, together with a large central pit that might have been used for grain storage.

At Skara Brae and Rinyo in the Orkney Islands, where timber is scarce, houses were built completely of stone, as was the furniture that they contained (Fig. 23). Beds, cupboards and storage boxes were all fashioned from slabs of the local stone. This made conditions at Skara Brae quite different from anything that might be found elsewhere in Britain. The owners of these houses bred cattle and sheep, but did not grow crops. Skara Brae was preserved when a storm buried it under sand dunes, where it remained until the middle of the last century. Pottery at Skara Brae and Rinyo is thick and coarse, and decorated with deep grooved patterns. Vessels of the same kind are found at the henge monuments in southern England. On the whole Late Neolithic pottery is much thicker than in Early Neolithic times and is heavily decorated with bone- and cord-impressed patterns.

23 The interior of Hut 1 at Skara Brae in the Orkney Islands. You can see the stone dresser, box-beds and central hearth

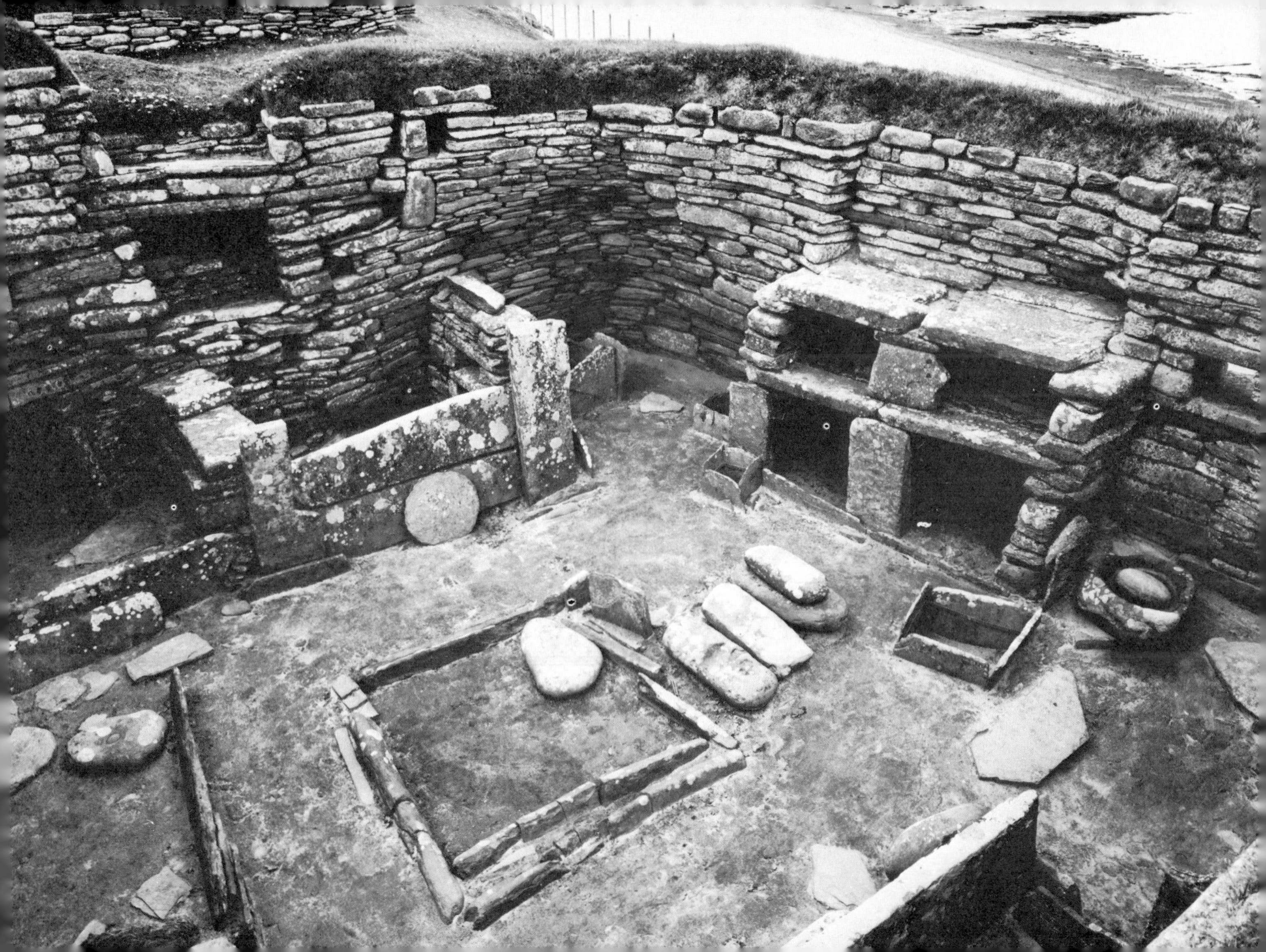

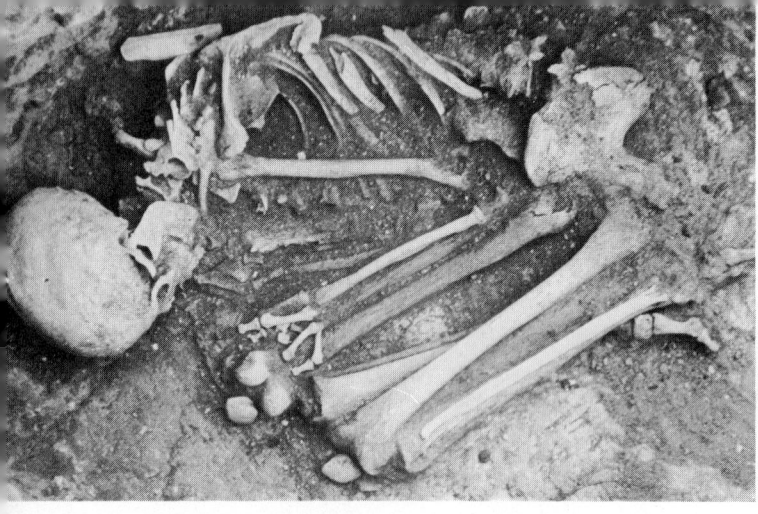

24 A crouched burial of Late Neolithic date, found under a round barrow at Dunstable in Bedfordshire. There is a flint knife beside the shoulder blade

25 A bell-beaker (*left*) from Roundway Down and a long-necked beaker from Durrington (both Wiltshire)

Burial ideas were beginning to change and small round barrows were built in various parts of Britain containing burials in a crouched-up position (Fig. 24), Neolithic pottery and flint work. The reason was probably new influences from the continent of Europe, and between 2500 and 2300 BC fresh groups of farmers, from the mouth of the river Rhine, arrived in eastern England. Not only did these people look different from the native farmers, having shorter, rounder heads, but they brought with them a distinctive type of drinking vessel known as a bell-beaker, which is found in their graves. The earlier Neolithic people had much longer, narrower skulls.

The bell-beakers were made of biscuit-thin clay, usually orange in colour, and were decorated in two ways. Some had patterns on the outside made by twisted cord pressed into the wet clay. The others had many narrow bands of decoration filled in with triangles and diamond shapes that had been made with a small wooden or flint comb pressed into the fabric. Vessels with the twisted cord decoration are mostly found in northern England, whilst the comb-impressed ones belong in the south (Fig. 25). Very few settlements of the Bell-Beaker People have been found, but where houses are known they are usually small and oval or circular in plan. Their graves, too, are circular, and contain only one body, which lies with knees drawn up to the chin. It is often accompanied by pieces of a beaker, buttons of shale or jet, barbed-and-tanged flint arrow heads, stone wrist guards (for protecting the wrist against the flying bow-string) and copper knives (Fig. 26). A few graves also contain gold trinkets. It is clear that the Bell-Beaker Folk were the first to bring metal to Britain, though it is doubtful if they worked it themselves. They probably obtained it by way of occasional trade, which helps to explain its rarity at that time.

26 Typical contents of a Beaker grave. A long-necked beaker, a riveted bronze dagger, an archer's wrist-guard, barbed-and-tanged flint arrowheads, a shale button, a stone battle-axe and flint dagger

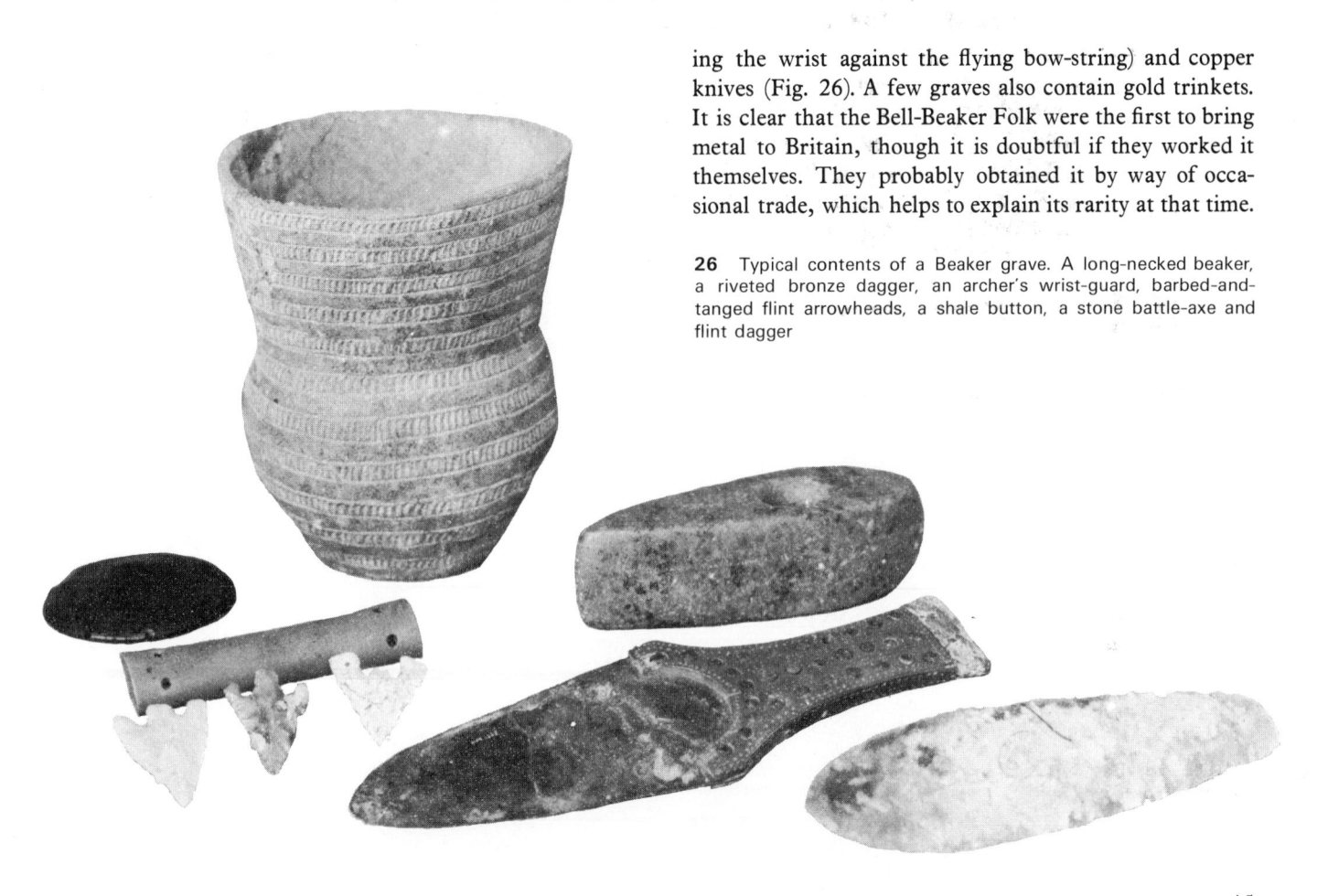

Somewhere between 2200 and 2100 BC another series of invasions of Beaker Folk began that lasted for several centuries. They were more complicated than the first, and archaeologists have discovered that at least five separate groups of settlers came to Britain. Some from the middle Rhineland settled in Wessex, and along the east coast as far north as the Scottish lowlands. Three others occupied Yorkshire, East Anglia and the Thames valley. Their beakers were taller and more slender than the earlier bell-beakers, and their decoration was much more varied. They are sometimes rather loosely called long-necked beakers. The new Beaker Folk could work in metal, and were the first people to produce bronze in Britain.

The discovery of metal had been made in the Near East, where gold was probably the first metal to be worked. It may have been the search for traces of gold in western Britain that brought the Beaker People to our country. Although gold is found as a pure metal, copper is not. It occurs as a blue or green ore in rocks, which have to be heated to a great temperature to produce copper as we know it. It may have been first discovered when pieces of ore were accidentally melted in a pottery kiln. Soon prospectors were searching for it in the ore-bearing rocks of the west. The melted ore could be poured into moulds carved out of stone, and copper axe-heads and knives could be mass-produced. Copper was very expensive and used only by chieftains. It was not as tough as the Beaker Folk would have liked and it tended to curl at the edges. By adding a small portion of tin ore to the copper (about a tenth) they produced bronze, which was much tougher and even more suitable for axes and a host of other objects.

The Beaker Folk continued to use the henge monuments, but adapted them to their own use. Often they erected circles of stones inside them, as at Avebury in Wiltshire. Outside they sometimes laid out avenues of stones in rows. Sometimes they constructed even more complicated features like the great arrangements of stones at Stonehenge (Fig. 29). This famous circle was changed a number of times. You can still see the bank and ditch of the first monument today with, outside it, the earliest stone, called the Heel Stone (Fig. 27). This was the only stone to be set up at first, and it may have indicated the position of sunrise on Midsummer Day. The Beaker Folk improved on this by bringing long, narrow 'Bluestones' from the Prescelly mountains (which they may have considered to be sacred) in South Wales, and carrying them on rafts and sledges to Wiltshire, where they were set up in a double circle at the centre of Stonehenge to form what archaeologists call Stonehenge period 2 (Fig. 28). Later in the Bronze Age the Welsh stones were taken down and used in a different way, described in the next chapter.

You can see another fine henge monument with stones inside it at Arbor Low in Derbyshire. In many parts of

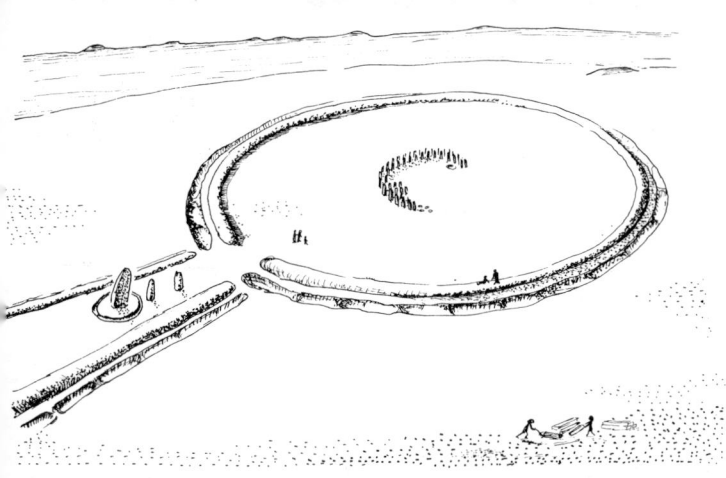

27 The Heel Stone was the first stone to be set up at Stonehenge. Unlike all the other stones it has not been artificially shaped in any way

top **28** The bluestone Stonehenge in Period 2
bottom **29** An aerial view of Stonehenge. Its surrounding bank and ditch can be clearly seen, as well as the final arrangement of stones at its centre

47

30 A row of Bronze Age round barrows at Taphouse near Broadoak in Cornwall

Britain the Beaker Folk set up stone circles on their own without surrounding henges. There is Stanton Drew in Somerset, and in Cornwall you can see the Hurlers and Merry Maidens and many more. Oxfordshire has the Rollright Stones, Derbyshire the Nine Ladies, and Cumberland Long Meg and her Daughters, and Castlerigg (Fig. 31). Country folk have given them a rich variety of names and invented some splendid legends about kings and knights and maidens all turned to stone.

In recent years mathematicians and astronomers have tried to find some order and purpose in the stone circles. They have shown that they were sometimes laid out using a unit of length that they call a megalithic yard (2.720 feet or 746 millimetres) which is equal to a man's average pace. Some of the circles were possibly used for observing the movements of the moon and for predicting eclipses, but a number of bold claims have been made that Neolithic man had a vast knowledge of astronomy and geometry, some of which are almost as wild as the legends of the witches and wandering stones.

Around the stone circles one can often see the burial mounds of the Beaker Folk and their Bronze Age successors, round bowl-barrows covering crouched skeletons (see Fig. 35). Perhaps we may compare them with graveyards by our parish churches (Fig. 30). Around Stonehenge are some of the finest barrow cemeteries in England, although many of the barrows date from the early Bronze Age. The most amazing barrow of all is near Avebury at Silbury Hill. There the Late Neolithic people built a mound which they enlarged several times, till it eventually reached a height of 40 metres and covered 2.2 hectares of land (as much as 22 football pitches!). Although the centre of Silbury has been excavated, no burial is known to have been found.

31 This stone circle at Castlerigg near Keswick in Cumberland was probably set up by the Beaker folk

7 · Chieftains and Peasants: the Bronze Age

2100 BC to 700 BC

32 Bronze Age pottery. A collared urn from Wilsford (Wiltshire) and two 'pygmy' cups — the rear one called an Aldbourne cup, from Wimbourne St Giles (Dorset), and a grape cup at the front, from Upton Lovell (Wilts)

There was no particular day when the Neolithic period ended and the Bronze Age began: the change was very gradual indeed, and took place very slowly in different parts of Britain. Scattered throughout the country were groups of Late Neolithic farmers and the Beaker Folk. Some had mixed and married, some still lived in isolated groups. As a result, a variety of pottery and metal types are found at the start of the Bronze Age. As well as late beakers and Neolithic pottery there were large-collared urns, highly decorated 'food vessels', tiny 'pygmy' cups, and numerous other related pots (Fig. 32). Although most metal in our part of the world was produced in Ireland, England seems to have had its own centres of production, where flat axes, riveted knives and daggers, amongst other items, were made.

In southern England, in particular, metal working developed on a grand scale, and for a short time a fairly small group of people grew rich on the proceeds. Because of its wealth this group stands out from all the others. It is loosely called the Wessex Culture, and we know of it from finds, mainly from Wiltshire, Dorset, Hampshire and Berkshire, of bronze daggers with blades riveted to their hilts, a wide variety of gold objects, jewellery of amber and faience (a form of blue glass), and pottery and flint work. It is the gold that makes the Wessex Culture distinct from those in the rest of Britain in the early Bronze Age. The gold objects consist of diamond-shaped plates (one 18 cm long, the others 3 cm long) that must have been sewn on to clothing, large conical gold-covered shale buttons, amber discs bound with gold, and gold beads, pendants and belt-hooks. It has been suggested that this was all the work of a single master goldsmith working somewhere in southern England. On the other hand hundreds of tiny gold pins used to decorate the hilts and pommels of daggers, and some of the daggers themselves, are very like examples found in Brittany; in 1938 it was considered that the chieftains of the Wessex Culture had strong links with Brittany, and might even have moved to Britain from there. How they acquired their wealth is uncertain, but they probably controlled the bronze-making industry. This must also have involved exporting metal objects to Europe, and importing stone battle axes and Scandinavian amber, which was used for making jewellery. Amongst the more unusual objects are a gold cup found at Rillaton in Cornwall and a 'sceptre' or 'mace' with a bone-decorated handle and stone head from Bush Barrow near Stonehenge in Wiltshire (Figs. 33 & 34). A number of Wessex burial mounds contain the curious little pygmy or incense cups, which may have held sacred embers used to light funeral fires.

33 The Rillaton gold cup, 8·2 cm high (in the British Museum)

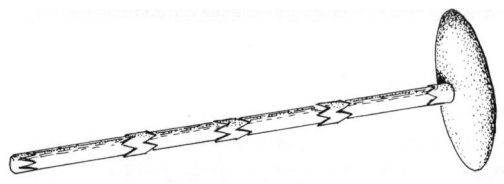

34 The Bush Barrow mace, or sceptre, in Devizes Museum

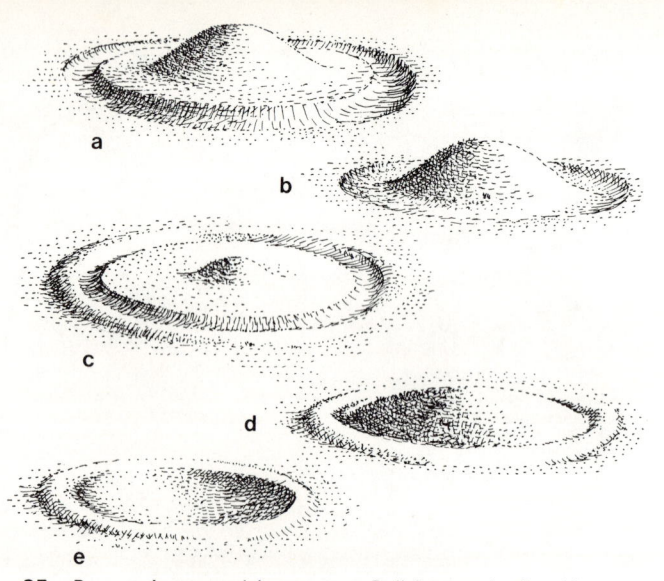

35 Bronze Age round barrows **a.** Bell barrow **b.** Bowl barrow **c.** Disc barrow **d.** Saucer barrow **e.** Pond barrow

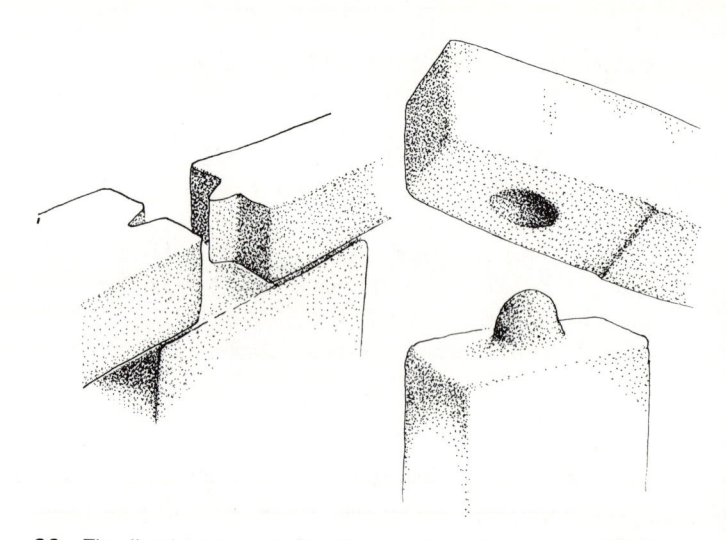

36 The lintel stones of Stonehenge dovetailed together (*left*) and attached to the upright stones by mortice and tenon joints (*right*)

Cemeteries of round barrows spread rapidly throughout Britain during the Early Bronze Age, and must represent the burial places of whole families or tribes over many years, but in Wessex they took on special shapes (Fig. 35). The most imposing were the bell-barrows, which covered bodies usually buried in a crouching position and often accompanied by weapons – arrowheads, bronze daggers and stone battle axes. These barrows had large central mounds surrounded by a flat, narrow ledge or berm, and enclosed by a ditch. Other bodies, often those of women, were cremated and placed at the centres of disc-barrows. Here a tiny mound stood near the middle of a flat circular platform, again surrounded by a ditch and outer bank. As well as these two main types of barrow there were some less common types, including saucer and pond barrows, that contained the bodies of men, women and children. The saucer barrow has a broad, low mound, the pond barrow is hollowed out like a pond.

Perhaps the most outstanding achievement of the

37 Part of the great sarsen stone circle of Stonehenge. The smaller stones inside are the bluestones brought from Wales

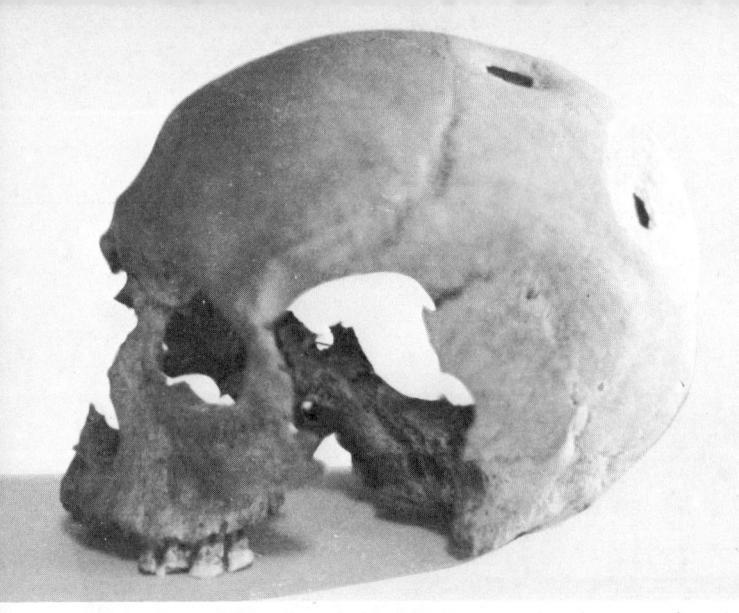

38 A Bronze Age skull showing two trepanning operations

Wessex chieftains was the remodelling of Stonehenge, using a hard local sandstone called sarsen, and the setting up of the five great sarsen stone trilithons at the centre. These were each made of two upright stones and one across the top forming an arch. Surrounding them were a continuous circle of sarsen stones dovetailed and morticed together (Fig. 36), with the re-used Welsh bluestones in a circle and horseshoe arrangement between them (Fig. 37). No one doubts that these were carefully set up on a central line that passes through the older Heel Stone and faces the midsummer sunrise and midwinter sunset, although some of the other astronomical and mathematical claims made for the circle and its builders are open to considerable doubt. This third period of Stonehenge can be dated to about 1800 BC. It is particularly noticeable that a great number of cemeteries of Wessex Culture barrows lie along the chalk ridges around Stonehenge.

Most people who lived in Britain in the Early Bronze Age were buried in round barrows of bowl type. Here a central grave was covered with a mound of earth that might have been dug from a surrounding ditch or scraped from the land nearby (Fig. 35). Clearly the old Beaker method of burial was still in use. Sometimes the burial ceremony seems to have required baskets of soil from a number of different places to be dumped on to the barrow mound. Some of these barrows were surrounded by circles of wooden stakes or posts, or these were built into the earth mound. Perhaps they marked off a sacred burial area before the earth was piled up. Some barrows had small stone-walled cists (or graves) at their centres, whilst others contained massive coffins hollowed out of tree-trunks. One such coffin had held a corpse wrapped in animal furs. Just before its burial a single stem of flowering hedge-parsley had been dropped into the coffin.

From graves like this we can tell a great deal about the people who are buried in them. Many men were buried with a number of arrowheads and a wrist-guard, indicating that they were archers with sheaves of arrows. Two or

54

39 Reconstruction of a Bronze Age family group

three graves have been found with the heads of hawks in them, suggesting that falconry was practised. Perhaps the most remarkable discoveries in early Bronze Age graves are indications of prehistoric brain surgery (Fig. 38). Skeletons exhibiting the scars of trepanning operations, in which circular discs of bone were cut from the skull with a flint blade, have been found a number of times. We imagine that this was done to relieve pressure on the brain, perhaps epilepsy, and to let out evil spirits. It is quite amazing that some people survived the experience, and more than one lived to have six or seven operations.

Although only traces of Bronze Age clothes have survived in England, whole costumes have been preserved in the Danish peat bogs, and from these we can see that they were made of fur and animal hair, wool or nettle fibres (Fig. 39). Men dressed in knee-length tunics that hung from beneath their arm-pits, secured with belts round the waists, and cloaks over their shoulders that might be held in place with pins. Some wore trousers, and at least one wore some kind of gaiters with two buttons on either leg. On their heads they sometimes wore round woollen hats, rather like padded tea-cosies, and on their feet simple leather shoes or boots. The women usually wore woollen jerseys and skirts, sometimes with cloaks, which they might secure with buttons of jet or shale. Their hair was held in place with bone hair pins, and they were often buried with small bronze awls that may have been connected with leather working, or

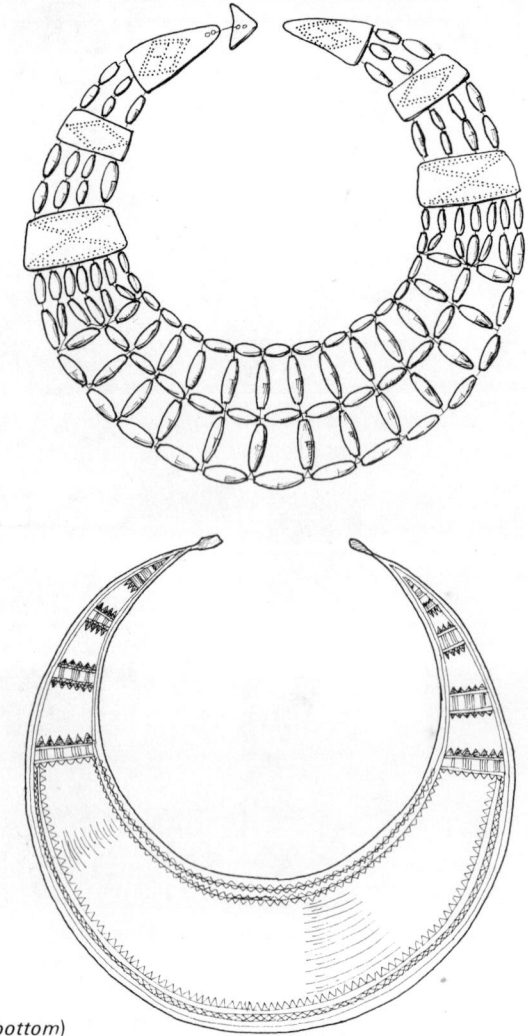

40 An amber necklace (*top*) and a gold lunula, or collar (*bottom*)

even tattooing – perhaps to enhance their beauty. Some women and young men wore bronze or gold ear-rings, or had jet studs inserted through the lobes of their ears.

Large pots called collared urns appeared at the end of the Neolithic period all over England. At first they were used for storing food, but during the Early Bronze Age they were used more and more as containers for the ashes of the dead. They have deep decorated collars, often with necks, which made it easier to lift them, or to tie cloths over their mouths. Sometimes the urns have been found in graves, upside down with their mouths sealed with clay, perhaps to keep the spirit of the dead inside.

Heavily decorated rounded bowls called, for want of a better name, food-vessels, were also being made in the early Bronze Age, mainly in the north and north-west. These were placed in graves alongside burials and may have contained food and drink for the dead. It is clear that the makers of the food-vessels were influenced by the old pottery styles of the Peterborough pots and beakers. In the same graves men were often buried with daggers of bronze, their blades protected by leather scabbards or wrapped in moss. Women were accompanied by crescent-shaped necklaces of jet and shale in which rows of beads were separated by rectangular spacer plates (Fig. 40). In Wessex similar necklaces were made of amber, and the

41 The Middle Bronze Age farm on Itford Hill, Sussex. The chieftain's hut may have been the one from which smoke is rising

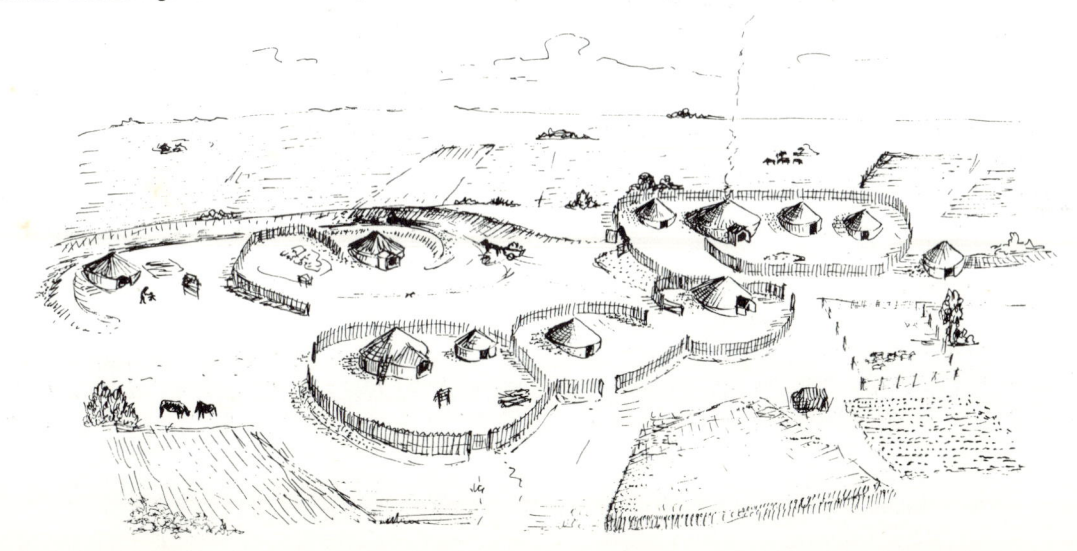

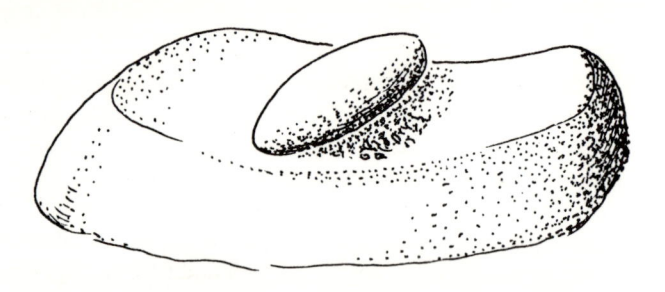

42 A saddle quern and a rotary quern

shape was copied in Ireland in the form of gold *lunulae* or collars, some of which were exported to Britain and the Continent (Fig. 40). The food-vessel makers seem to have had direct connections with Ireland, where some of their pots are found in stone-lined graves or cists, which are sometimes decorated with simple patterns pecked into the stone, called cup-and-ring marks. These marks are found not only in northern Britain and Ireland, but as far away as Spain and Portugal.

Most of the Bronze Age people were farmers, growing barley for grain and ale, and breeding sheep, cattle, goats and pigs. They lived in many parts of Britain, not in large villages, but in single round houses or small groups of huts. Although many of these settlements have been recognized, only a small number have been excavated. One of the most thoroughly examined, dating from the Middle Bronze Age, was on Itford Hill in Sussex. Eleven round huts ranging in diameter from 4.5 to 6 metres, and built of a ring of posts with clay walls and thatched roofs, were enclosed within small yards (Fig. 41). The settlement was approached by a hollow or sunken roadway, and was surrounded by small square fields. One of the huts was larger than the others, and may have been used by the headman, whilst the very small ones might have been for storage and animals. Ninety metres north of the settlement was the cemetery; a low round barrow covered the cremated bones of a middle-aged man, and the remains of sixteen cremations had been buried in nearby ground on the village side, some in old and damaged urns. Hundreds of flint flakes were littered over the surface of the cemetery, which suggests that this was a favourite spot for flint knapping.

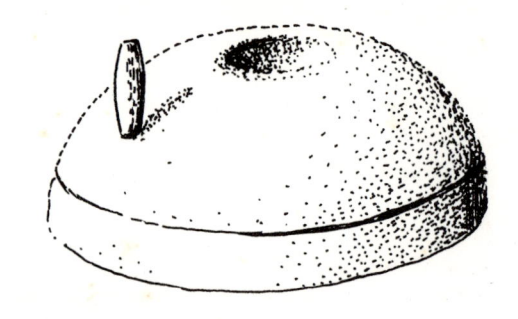

The Bronze Age ploughs cut a single furrow, and the criss-cross pattern of the marks that they made has been found at a number of British sites. The farmers stored their grain in covered pits in the ground during the winter. They saved some for the next year's sowing, but most of it was eaten. The seeds could be ground into flour by rubbing them between the two stones of a saddle-quern. This consisted of a long saddle-shaped lower stone, and a round upper stone. These saddle-querns were not terribly efficient and the flour they produced was coarse and always gritty (Fig. 42).

A major change took place at the beginning of the Middle Bronze Age when the elaborate burials of the earlier period were suddenly and dramatically replaced by cremations in large pottery urns. As we have seen, there had certainly been some cremation before, but now it became acceptable for everyone, and the burial of objects with the dead almost ceased. This is particularly unfortunate for archaeologists looking for material to date the burials. Why, one wonders, did it happen? There is nothing to suggest the arrival of new people in Britain. It must have been the result of new ideas amongst the Middle Bronze Age people, but unfortunately this is the sort of question that it is almost impossible for archaeology to answer. For some time the ashes and bones continued to be buried under barrows, though quite often they were put into urns which were inserted into existing mounds. Eventually, as we have seen at Itford Hill, the urns were placed in flat cemeteries; these may have been marked in some manner that has since been destroyed. Few remains of the actual cremation pyres have been found: we may assume that they were near the cemeteries and required a lot of timber or peat to fire them.

New metal work appeared during the Middle Bronze Age: dirks and rapiers took the place of daggers with riveted hilts, palstaves replaced flat and flanged axes, and spearheads with a hollow socket down the centre were found more efficient than the earlier tanged types (Figs 43 and 44). Such weapons required great skill in their manufacture. Some were cast in moulds carved from stone, in which two identical halves fitted together to make the shape of the final object. Others were made by using what is called the 'lost wax' method. A complicated metal design was first modelled in beeswax, and then coated with clay, leaving an opening at one end. The clay was heated and the wax melted and ran out, leaving the impression of the object baked into the clay. Molten metal was next poured into the mould, which took on the shape of the wax impression. When it had cooled the clay was broken away and the metal implement remained. You can try this method by using candle-grease and clay, and pouring plaster of Paris, instead of metal, into the mould.

Farming settlements occur in many parts of Britain, particularly on the chalk hills of the south. At Itford Hill roadways and tracks wandered over the downs, linking the small groups of huts that formed single farmsteads. Sometimes such farms were surrounded by banks, ditches and palisades, but these served to keep animals and small children from straying and wild animals out, rather than for defence. At Shearplace Hill in Dorset such a farm seems to have consisted of two houses, one for the family and one for the animals. Close by was a sheltered hollow where grain could be threshed, and a pond where the animals could drink. Near these were a small stock-pen, and a larger paddock that might have been ploughed. It was approached by a sunken road or hollow-way that ran through numerous small fields. The people of Shearplace Hill used large coarse bucket-shaped pots, often decorated with bands of designs made by pressing the finger-tips on the soft clay. Such urns are called Deverel-Rimbury urns, after two places where they were found. They were used not only for household purposes, but as containers for cremation burials, as often happened in prehistory. Settlements like Shearplace Hill lasted right through the Late Bronze Age and into the Iron Age without much change, and one gets the impression that England was a peaceful place where little happened for a very long time.

In the stone countryside of Dartmoor and Exmoor small villages were constructed of stone, and very often their foundations still survive and are worth visiting. One of the best known is Grimspound on Dartmoor, where a large thick wall (partly restored) encloses a number of circular huts, some with fireplaces and porches. On the surrounding hillside you can still make out the shapes of the small square and rectangular fields, marked by low banks of stones and earth.

43 Bronze Age metal work **a.** riveted dagger **b.** dirk with metal hilt **c.** tanged spearhead **d.** socketed spearhead

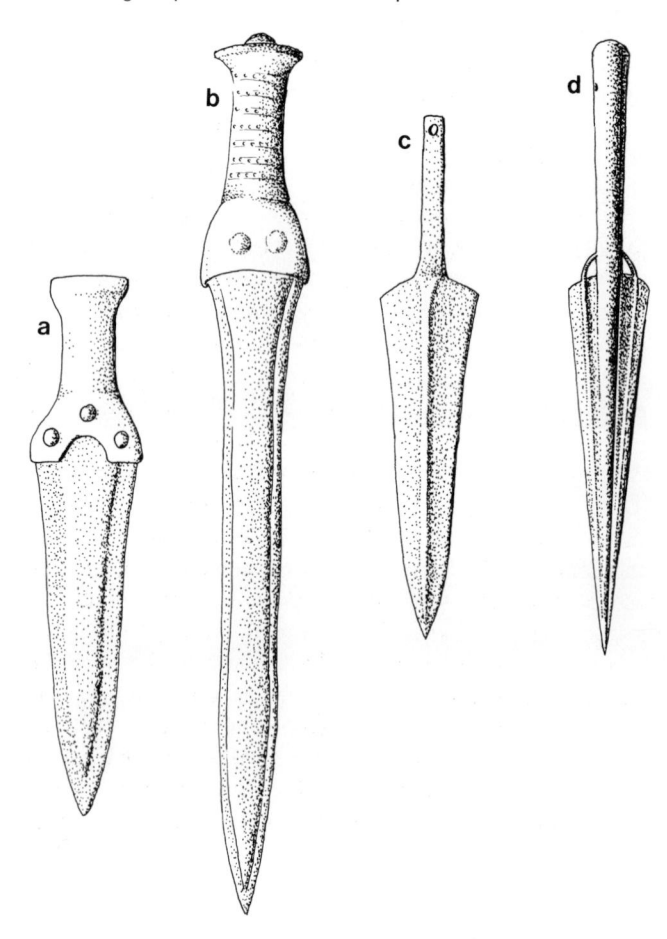

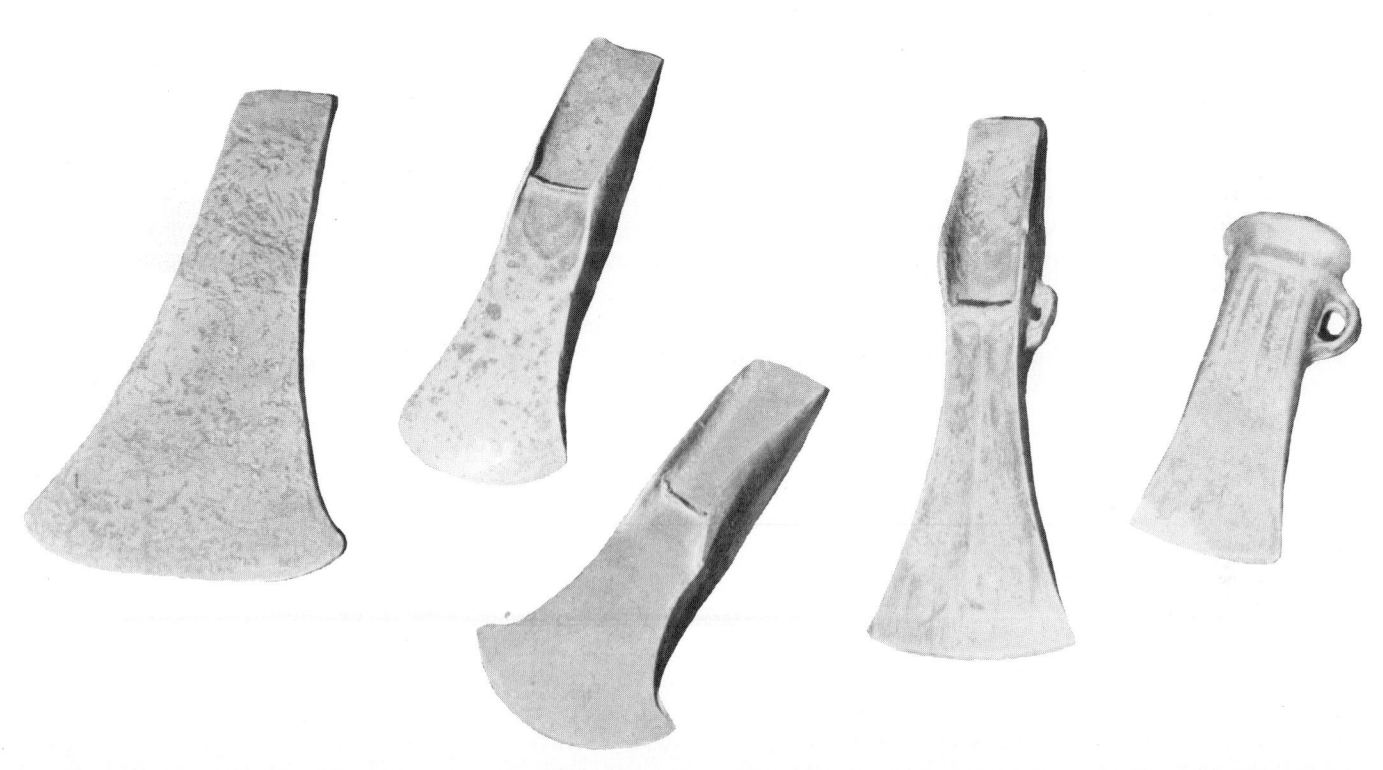

44 The development of bronze axes. A flat axe on the left, three flanged axes in the centre (one with a loop for a safety cord) and a palstave on the right

8 · *Farms and Fortresses: the Early and Middle Iron Age* 700 BC to 400 BC, 400 BC to 100 BC

Like the Bronze Age, the Iron Age has no really obvious beginning. Somewhere about 700 years before Christ a few rare objects made of iron found their way into Britain from Europe, brought here no doubt by traders. At first they were jealously guarded by their proud owners, but as time went by more were introduced and soon the natives were making them themselves. This didn't mean that bronze, copper and flint ceased to be used, but, as with plastic in our own times, old objects were made more cheaply and efficiently in the new material. There are very few counties in Britain that do not have small iron deposits, and we can assume that iron working was developed locally in many places.

Farming was still the mainstay of Iron Age life, and all over southern Britain small, isolated farmsteads were constructed. Two or three huts, usually circular, were surrounded by a palisade, and approached by trackways through the fields. At last the wheel had reached Britain, and it was not long before man found a number of uses for it. The farmers made carts, which enabled them to move their products with greater ease. Ploughs were used, pulled by oxen, to till small squarish fields on the downs and moorlands. These are known as Celtic fields, because the Iron Age folk belonged to a great European group of people called the Celts. Sometimes the ploughing went along the slope of the hills, creating some of the stepped lynchets that we see on the hillsides. (Others may be of Saxon or medieval date.) They are made by the soil creeeping slowly downhill and piling up against an obstruction such as a fence or wall to form a step or lynchet. Boundary ditches were often dug between fields and may have separated one farmer's holding from the next: sometimes, of course, they were used for drainage.

Within the farmstead itself stood a main living hut, often about 12 metres in diameter, with a low-pitched conical roof supported by four central posts, and probably thatched with reeds or turf. At the centre was a hearth with a flat cooking slab beside it. Most of the light came from the door, which had a porch to give shelter from the wind and rain. Outside in the yard would be similar huts for other members of the family, or for animals and equipment.

On chalk or limestone land the farmers used pits about 1.5 metres deep, and about 1 metre in diameter to store grain during the winter. It was covered with a basket-work lid, and could be kept in good condition as seed for the next year or for grinding into flour. At the farmstead of Little Woodbury in Wiltshire more than 360 pits were dug, but it is clear that only two or three were used at a time. After a few years they became soured and infected with mildew, so they were filled in and new ones dug. Other pits were used to collect water, or as latrines and for refuse. Wooden racks were used for drying hay or ears of corn.

The everyday equipment of the farm would have included a rotary quern, in which a circular upper stone revolved on a lower one: these were a great improvement on the older saddle-querns and are still in use in some remote parts of north-west Britain today (see Fig. 42). Pottery in the early Iron Age was generally still home-made from coils of clay and was often bucket-shaped, although finer wares were now being produced, sometimes lightly decorated with chevron (inverted V) patterns, and their surfaces burnished by polishing them with bones before firing. These were made by specialist potters who traded them round the country. Wooden vessels were also made, although we are not certain when the lathe was introduced into Britain; and probably wooden buckets and barrels made of staves were used. Metal buckets and cauldrons were first made in the late Bronze Age, and for the first time the inhabitants of Britain could boil food over a fire instead of merely roasting it on a spit. They almost certainly drank some form of ale brewed from barley, mead produced from honey and spices, and perhaps cider made from wild apples; all these made a change from water or milk. They probably ate cheese with unleavened bread (a dough mixture without yeast).

One can imagine the interior of an Iron Age hut on a winter's evening, filled with smoke and lighted by a flickering fire. At the centre a great cauldron of stew bubbles above the hearth. Dogs lurk in the shadows, ready to pounce on any morsel of meat or bone that may come their way. A baby cries in a hammock strung between two of the roof supports. Children rolled in furs and blankets sleep snugly on a pile of bracken under the low eaves of the roof. A woman is weaving cloth in a chequered pattern using home-produced wool whilst another grinds corn on the rotary mill. Her husband fits a new handle to his axe and strengthens the sling that he uses to drive off the wild animals that attack his flocks. A young man is plucking the feathers from a duck that he has caught by the river, whilst a girl is coiling clay to form a new jar. Skins hung across the wooden doors keep out the draughts and make the house stuffy and cosy.

An unusual Iron Age village existed at Glastonbury in Somerset, where about 150 BC a number of square or rectangular timber-framed houses were built on wooden piles above the edge of a lake. A similar village

45 A hillfort palisade of wood, with turf and timber piled behind it

existed nearby at Meare, but because of just two examples we shouldn't get the idea that everyone in Iron Age Britain lived in raised houses on the edge of lakes. The occupants used boats hollowed out from tree-trunks, and fished in the surrounding waters. They also seem to have kept animals on the shores and ploughed the nearby fields.

During the Late Bronze Age the first hilltop forts were built. In the beginning these were little more than farms protected by a palisade, but with the additional advantage of a high viewpoint and sturdy gate. As time passed the owners made them stronger by digging ditches around the hilltop and piling the excavated soil into a high bank behind the palisade. When the Iron Age began, a number of these small hillforts existed in Britain; they had presumably been made as defence against greedy neighbours who had started to seize land, cattle and sheep by force. A number of immigrant groups moved into Scotland from Europe, and they probably brought with them many ideas for fortification which had started there. Other methods were probably invented independently in our country.

Hillforts were built in a number of ways, but in the early Iron Age most required a massive timber defence consisting of two parallel rows of posts sunk into the solid sub-soil, and linked together with tie-beams (Fig. 45). This box shape was filled with soil and rubble from a deep V-shaped ditch, from which it was separated by a narrow ledge or berm. Archaeologists call this type of structure a Hollingbury-type rampart, after the fort in Sussex where it was first studied. The amount of timber required for such a fort would be enormous. Apart from the main upright posts, each 15 to 20 centimetres in diameter and 3 metres high at least, there would have been hundreds of tie-beams and facing posts, attached either vertically or horizontally. In stone areas the ramparts were often faced with dry-stone walls, but even these sometimes required timber strengthening.

The builders paid particular attention to entrances, which were always the weakest part of any defence. Some were of a simple straight-through type with a wooden gate and nothing else, but more often the ends of the rampart were turned inwards like a funnel with gates at the inner and outer ends of it (Fig. 46). The enemy could

46 A hillfort entrance

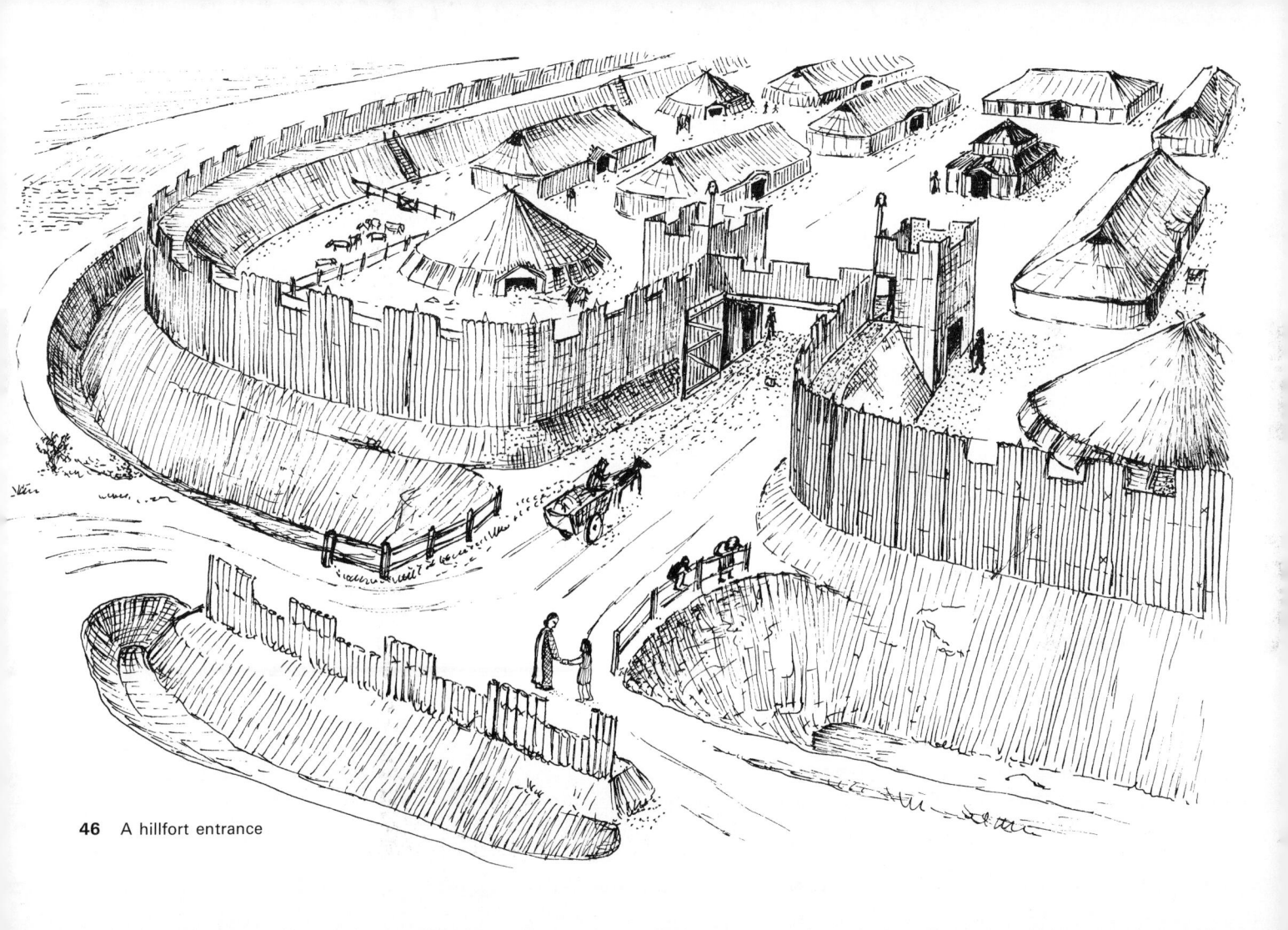

47 The massive banks and ditches of Maiden Castle in Dorset. This great hillfort is one of the finest in Britain

be seen from the adjoining rampart ends and dealt with accordingly. Such gateways may have had a bridge forming a sentry walk, or even a tower, above them. We are not sure exactly how the gates were hung, since no iron hinges have ever been found, and some people think they may have been suspended and lowered from above like a stage curtain, or swung up and down like a draw-bridge. But probably they opened like ordinary farm gates and had hinges that were made of a perishable material like leather which has left no trace.

Very few forts have obvious water supplies and we can only assume that they were occupied for very short periods and for that time water was kept in casks or buckets and perhaps clay-lined storage pits. Whilst some of the enclosures contain many huts and pits, others have only a single house. The two types must have had different purposes that we do not understand as yet. We must realize that to call all these sites 'forts' is misleading; they must have had many different uses.

Most hillforts were built on high hilltops from whence

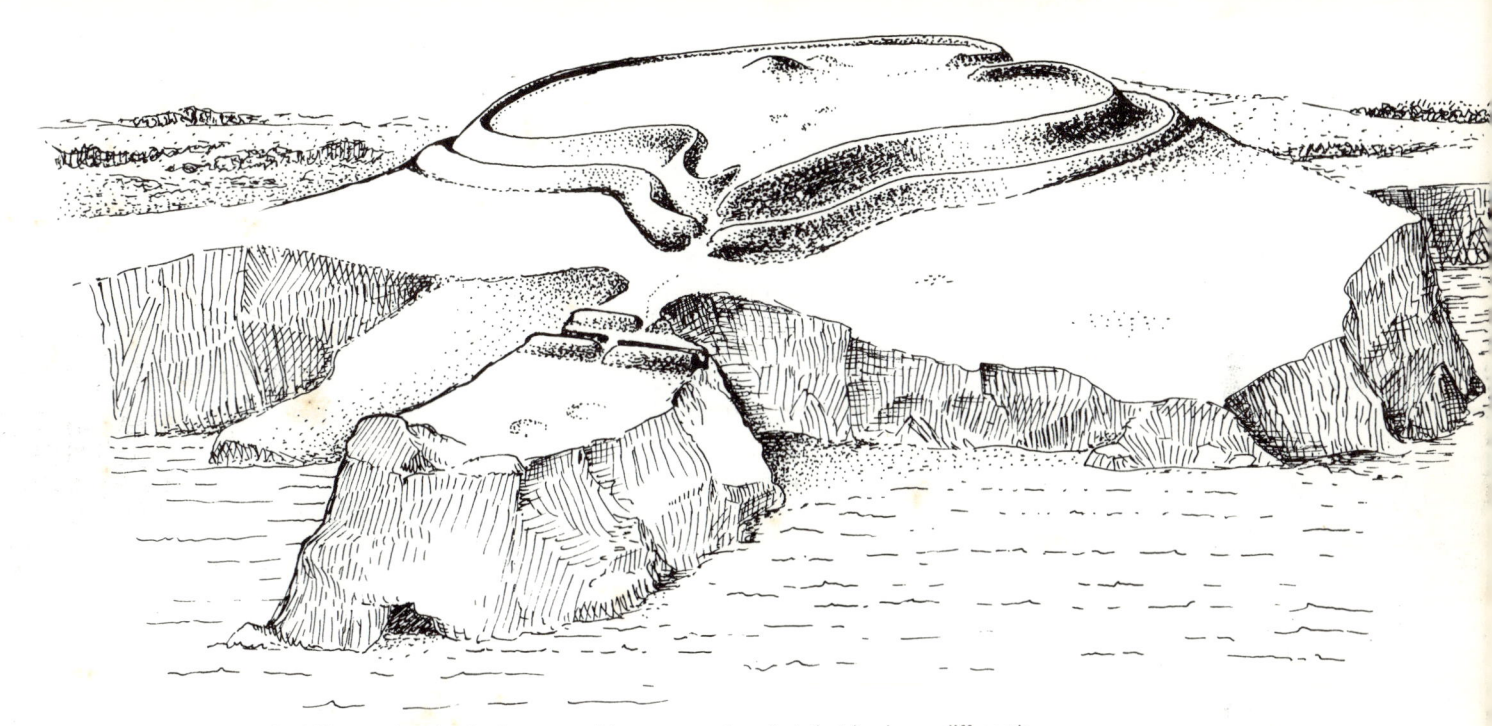

48 A contour fort on its hilltop today. In the foreground is a promontory fort that is also a cliff castle

the inhabitants could observe wide areas of countryside, though a few are found on low ground near rivers. Some have a single circuit of ramparts and ditches (univallate forts) whilst others have three or four circuits, one inside the other (multivallate) (Fig. 47). The defences of the major forts often follow the contour lines around the top of a prominent hill, and these are accordingly known as contour forts (Fig. 48). On lower ground where no suitable hills exist, or close to a river crossing, the forts tend to be circular or oval in plan but with extra-strong defences. These are the plateau forts.

In order to save labour Iron Age man sometimes

defended a hill-spur by simply building a line of defence across the neck of the spur and leaving the natural hill-slope to provide the rest of the protection. This resulted in a promontory fort. When this was done on the coast and a neck of land with steep cliffs jutted into the sea the fort produced is called a cliff-castle.

One kind of fort that doesn't fit into any of these groups is known as a hill-slope fort. These are found in south-western England; they lie half-way down the slopes of hills and seem to have been used as pens for cattle. The interior is often divided up into a number of enclosures.

In eastern England forts of any kind are noticeably lacking and we may assume that some different way of life existed there in which they played little part.

Early forts were probably defended with the spear, which has a range of about 30 metres in skilled hands, with swords for close fighting. Bows and arrows don't seem to have been used at this time. Shields gave protection and probably most of them were made of wood covered with leather, though only the more ornate metal-covered examples have survived. The sling, with an effective range of 90 metres, was used throughout the Iron Age.

About 400 BC groups of people from France seem to have arrived in south-eastern England, bringing with them ideas for new, finer types of pottery bowls and more efficient daggers and safety-pin-type brooches. Both the pottery and metal-work were current in France at that time and came from a central European culture called La Tène after a hamlet in Switzerland. The new people arrived in the Thames valley and made their way into central and southern England. Whilst many apparently came in peace (since there is no evidence of their fighting), the native population saw them as potential enemies and strengthened and renewed their hillfort defences. In some parts of England they threw dykes across trackways to hold up the newcomers and mark the territory of the native farmers more clearly. At this time some of the Iron Age people from southern England moved north into Scotland in search of new lands of their own. Meanwhile some of the farmers who remained moved into the hillforts. From here they proceeded to control large areas of territory, and local tribal systems developed. As a result some of the forts became centres from which the territories were administered. Here could be found law and order, markets for cattle, food and merchandise of all sorts, and perhaps religious centres too. When the Romans arrived three centuries later they called these large administrative forts 'oppida'.

We know little of Iron Age religion. Burials, which tell us so much about earlier periods of prehistory, are entirely lacking for most of the Iron Age. If bodies were cremated then the ashes were scattered, for we do not find them buried in the ground. People may have tried to preserve the corpses by smoking or drying them and then placing them at some point in the village or fort where they could watch over the living, as still happens with some primitive peoples today. Some of the corpses may even have been eaten. After all, cannibalism is the most hygienic method of disposing of the dead! The Iron Age people seem to have believed in a nature goddess, who lived deep in the earth, and was responsible for making plants and animals grow. The Greeks called her Persephone, and we still talk of Mother Nature. Deep shafts were dug in the ground into which offerings and gifts were dropped as well as occasional animal and human sacrifices. Such shafts have been found in many parts of southern Britain and Europe. Springs too were considered to have special healing qualities for the sick, and hundreds of crude wooden statuettes of malformed human bodies have been deposited in pools, marshes and the sources of numerous rivers, most notably the Seine in France, where the moisture in the soil preserved them for archaeologists to find. We do not know if this was sympathetic magic or a thank offering to the god of the stream. Many of our rivers were given names in the Iron Age which have remained almost unchanged to the present day.

There are very few places in Britain where we have any Iron Age burials dated before 100 BC, but some have been found on the chalk hills around the village of Arras in Yorkshire. Here a tribe known as the Parisi, who had been driven out of France to Britain about

49 The skeleton of an Iron Age chieftain, buried with his chariot, and excavated in 1971 at Garton Slack in Yorkshire

250 BC, left cemeteries of small round barrows amongst which their chieftains were buried. Whilst the ordinary people were placed in graves with joints of pork, their leaders were often buried lying in their war chariots, accompanied by their horses, swords and shields (Fig. 49). Women of high position might be buried with a bronze mirror, often with a beautifully engraved backplate. The Parisi, perhaps more than the other Iron Age men in southern England, were great horsemen, and went to considerable lengths to decorate their horses with fine harness fittings of leather, bronze and enamel. It is interesting to observe that it was horsemen who made trousers the usual wear for all men, to make riding more comfortable. Previously only a few people had worn them.

69

9 · The End of Prehistoric Times: the Late Iron Age
100 BC to 43 AD

One of the most exciting features of the Middle and Late Iron Age was the appearance of a new art style which was used on metal work, pottery and wooden vessels.

In central Europe soon after 1000 BC the Iron Age people known as the Celts had expanded westwards and southwards to the Mediterranean, where they came into contact with the classical world. There they not only observed the customs of the Mediterranean but acquired a taste for its luxuries, including wine, as well as for its works of art. This taste developed as time went by and from the Etruscans, in particular, the Celts of Switzerland and France copied and adapted the simpler classical art motifs that they saw. Then they combined them with their own native art traditions, as well as various other ideas borrowed from the Orient and northern Europe, to create a new and characteristic style known as Celtic art, which flourished throughout the Middle and Late Iron Age and was also to reappear in the religious art of the Celtic church in the post-Roman period. It is best recognized by its flowing, curving lines based on the tendrils of plants, and the balanced, but not obviously symmetrical circular designs, lightly engraved on the back of mirrors (Fig. 50), sword scabbards and on

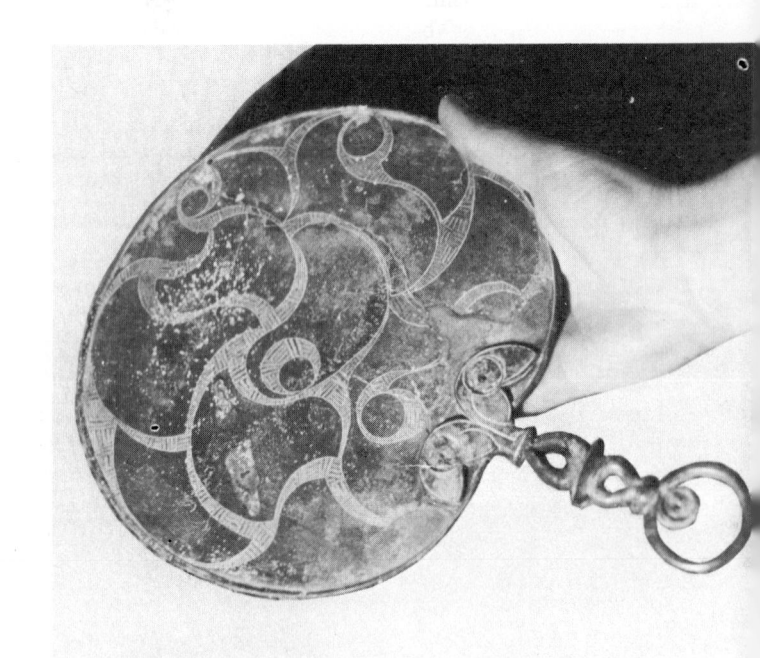

50 The engraved back of a Late Iron Age bronze mirror from Old Warden, Bedfordshire

51 A Late Iron Age bronze chariot-fitting decorated in the Celtic art style, from Cold Kitchen Hill, Brixton Deverill, Wilts. It probably guided the horses' reins

52 An iron firedog from a rich chieftain's grave, excavated at Baldock in Hertfordshire

numerous other articles (Fig. 51). Sometimes the design stands out in relief, having been hammered into the back of the bronze surface of a shield, or iron has been wrought to form the head of a fire-dog (Fig. 52). Occasionally its beauty is heightened by a skilful and restrained use of coloured enamel to highlight some part of the work.

71

53 The tribes of Britain in the Late Iron Age
V = Verulamium (St Albans)
C = Camulodunum (Colchester)

About 100 BC the relative peace of Britain was disturbed by the arrival on our eastern shores of groups of people from the area of modern Belgium, who are known as the Belgae. There are no settlements that can be dated to their first arrival, so perhaps they came first as traders or missionaries; they may even have been led by their scholars and priests, some of whom were known as Druids. Certainly the Belgae reintroduced the idea of cremating the dead and placing their ashes in wheel-made pottery urns. Sometimes these urns were placed in family cemeteries, around which low fences were set up to separate them from an adjoining group. Here is a clear change in religious outlook, and at first it occurs only in south-eastern England. A second group of Belgae who arrived fifty years later (about 50 BC) were clearly more warlike, and intended to obtain land and colonise southern Britain. In response to this threat the native tribesmen rebuilt their hillforts yet again and strengthened their ramparts, adding elaborate outworks at the gates, and preparing them for defence by their long-range weapon: the sling.

It is from about this time that prehistory and history overlap in England and for the first time we can learn the names of tribes and their leaders from the writings of the Greeks and Romans. By about 100 BC the people of southern England were organized into large units with territories occupying many hundreds of square miles. The map shows their approximate positions (Fig. 53).

The first Belgic people to arrive imposed themselves on the Cantiaci of Kent and then moved north to control the Catuvellauni, 'the mighty warriors' of Hertfordshire. When the second group of Belgae arrived they moved into Hampshire, Berkshire and west Sussex, where they were called the Atrebates and Regnenses.

The Belgic chieftain of the Catuvellauni was Cassivellaunus, and his is the first name we know from British history. He had a large hillfort somewhere in Hertfordshire. It was attacked by Julius Caesar in 54 BC, but Cassivellaunus survived and his territory was later increased by his son Cunobelin to stretch from St Albans to the Essex coast, thus absorbing the neighbouring Trinovantes. Their capital later moved from Prae Wood near St Albans to Camulodunum (Colchester).

The Atrebates were led by Commius, whose capital was on the site of Calleva Atrebatum (Silchester, Hampshire). They had no love for their eastern rivals, the Catuvellauni, and eventually sided with the Romans against them. Later, when Britain had been conquered by the Romans, Cogidubnus, a grandson of Commius, signed a treaty of friendship and allegiance with Rome that brought him the reward of a great palace at Fishbourne near Chichester.

The Belgic peoples brought the potters' wheel to Britain, which speeded up the making of pottery and improved the quality of the finished vessels (Fig. 54). Centres of pottery-making developed and the finished

54 Wheel-made Belgic pottery found at Camulodunum (Colchester)

pots were carried by cart or boat to many parts of the country. Potting as a home industry had largely come to an end. The lathe was used to turn wooden containers and to produce ornamental vases from shale. The Britons began to use light chariots for a single driver in battle and they managed them with a speed and skill which made the stoutest Roman heart quail (Fig. 55).

Both the Belgic groups minted coins of gold, silver and bronze. These they based on Greek originals which showed Philip of Macedon on one side and a horse and chariot on the reverse. It is interesting to see what a mess the Belgae made of copying these designs and how they

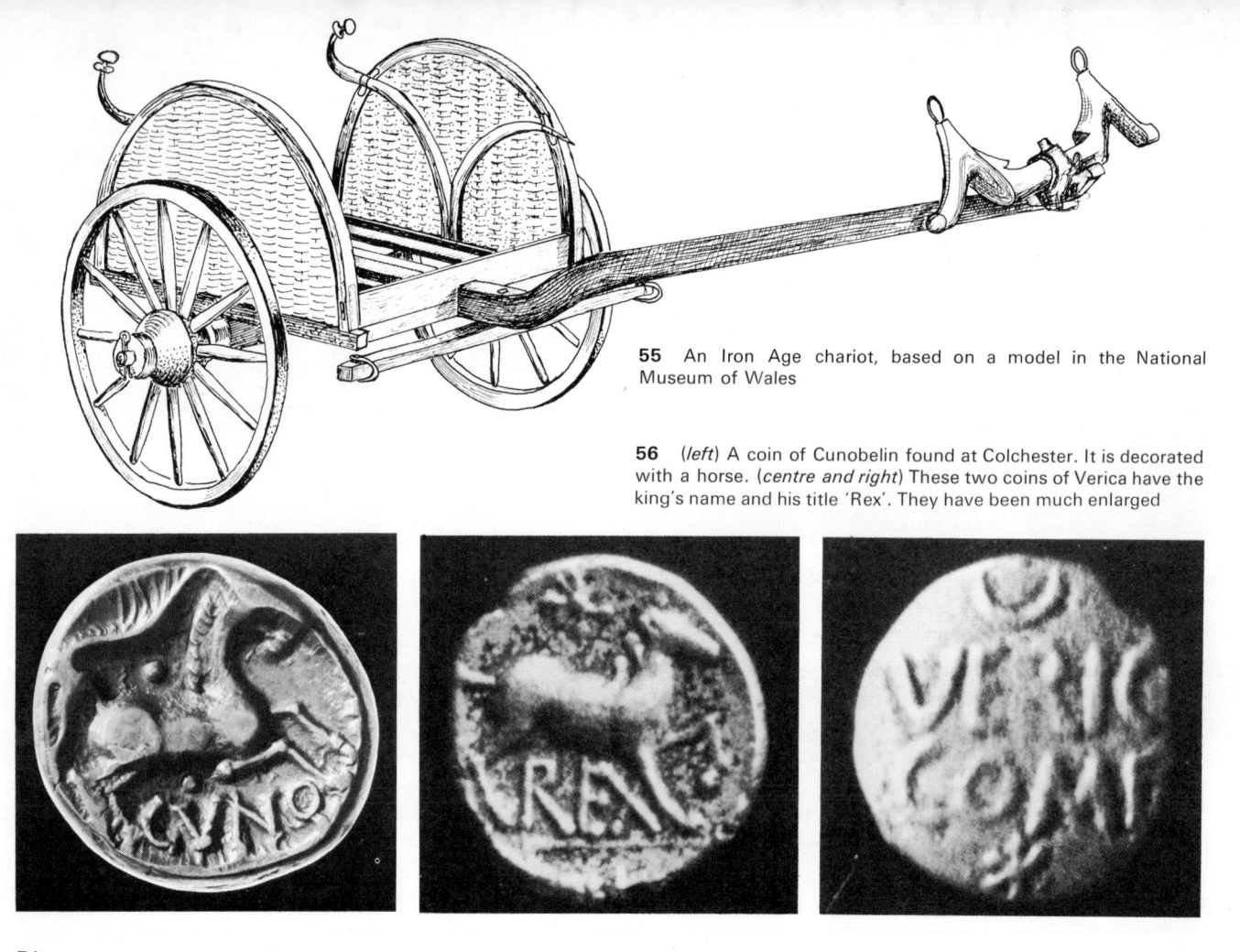

55 An Iron Age chariot, based on a model in the National Museum of Wales

56 (*left*) A coin of Cunobelin found at Colchester. It is decorated with a horse. (*centre and right*) These two coins of Verica have the king's name and his title 'Rex'. They have been much enlarged

grew less and less like the original as time passed. They wrote the names of their leaders in Roman letters on each coin and added the title REX (King) (Fig. 56).

When the Catuvellaunian rulers died their bodies were draped in rich clothing and jewellery and were burnt on cremation pyres. Their ashes, together with rich gifts, which might include couches, wine amphorae (jars), cauldrons, fire-dogs and spits (Fig. 52), cooking vessels, high-class pottery and glass, and musical instruments, were all placed in brick-lined burial vaults roofed with tiles, ready for an enormous party when the dead person reached the next world. A number of these rich tombs have been found in Hertfordshire and Bedfordshire, whilst at Lexden in Colchester the vault was buried under a large barrow. This one may well have been the tomb of King Addedomarus of the Trinovantes: the contents can be seen today in the Colchester Museum.

But there was more to the Late Iron Age in Britain than Belgic chieftains. These were the masters who expected work and service from the ordinary men and women. Farming still remained the most prominent means of making a living, but by this time farmers were producing surplus grain and cattle for export, together with hunting dogs and metal work. In return wine and oil, fine quality pottery, glass and bronzes were imported to swell the prestige of the ruling classes. By the end of the Iron Age class distinction had reared its head and come to stay. This point is made all the clearer by the finding of slave chains on a number of native British farms, and Caesar tells us that slaves, too, were exported from Britain. Boats from the Mediterranean brought goods to British shores, whilst the natives sailed along the coast in small, skin-covered boats called curraghs, which are still made in western Ireland today.

The lake-side village of Glastonbury was rebuilt about 50 BC on an artificial island or crannog. Round huts with wattle and daub walls were erected, with floors of clay. In this village pottery with flowing Celtic designs was used, and a variety of objects of wicker and wood have been found preserved in the damp soil, including baskets, tool handles, a ladder, doors, tubs, troughs, and parts of a wheel, as well as iron woodworking tools.

A series of groups had crossed from Europe to Scotland in the late eighth and seventh centuries BC. Amongst these were the Abernethy people, who built hillforts of stone in the north-east, with timber 'lacing' to tie the walls together. When these forts were deliberately set alight the timber in the walls was heated to such a temperature that it melted the adjoining stone work and 'vitrified' it into a solid mass.

In the north-west of Scotland, the Hebrides, the Shetlands and the Orkneys occur the curious tower structures known as brochs (Fig. 57). More than five hundred of these have been found. They consist of circular towers about 10.5 metres in diameter, narrowing towards the top, and rising to heights of between 6

57 The Broch of Mousa in Shetland

58 The entrance to one of the stone huts at Chysauster near Penzance in Cornwall. This Late Iron Age Village was occupied from about 100 BC until AD 250

and 12 metres. They have a single small entrance in their walls and narrow stairways that run upwards in the thickness of the walls to reach upper floor levels. It is assumed that they were occupied by single families and they were clearly designed for defence. Pottery found in the brochs resembles that of the earliest Iron Age, but specialized weaving combs and bobbins remind us that this is the sheep-rearing region of Britain and that already the wool and tweed industry was developing. Some of the cloth found its way south, even to the Roman Empire.

Britain during the last century before Christ had become a refuge for people fleeing from Roman rule. Many folk from France (or Gaul as it was called then) settled in southern England, and from there organized resistance to the Roman occupation of their homeland, and gave shelter to political refugees. This was one of the reasons why in 55 BC and 54 BC Julius Caesar mounted two expeditions to England. In the first he routed the Cantiaci of Kent, and on the second he reached the headquarters of Cassivellaunus in Hertfordshire and attacked it on two sides, but the Catuvellauni escaped on the third. These visits gave the Iron Age people a brief taste of Roman military power, but it was not until almost a hundred years later that the Claudian invasion of AD 43 brought England into the Roman Empire.

10 · Some Museums and Books and You

There are a great many museums in Britain and some of them have excellent collections of prehistoric material. A useful guide is published in July every year by ABC Travel Guides Ltd, called *Museums and Galleries in Great Britain and Ireland*. Copies of the latest edition can be obtained from most bookshops. Certainly everyone visiting London must see the prehistoric galleries at the British Museum and the Natural History Museum in South Kensington. In Scotland you should call at the National Museum of Antiquities in Queen Street, Edinburgh; and in Wales you will find the National Museum of Wales in Cathays Park, Cardiff, well worth a visit. Many of our other large towns and cities have excellent collections and mention can be made of Birmingham, Bristol, the Cambridge University Museum, Colchester, Exeter, Gloucester, Hereford, Hull, Leeds, Leicester, Manchester, Newcastle, Oxford (the Ashmolean Museum), Norwich, Reading and York. Some of the major prehistoric sites, like Avebury and Glastonbury, have museums nearby; and no one studying prehistoric Britain should fail to visit Devizes Museum in Wiltshire, which has one of the finest collections in Europe.

TAKING PART

There are archaeological societies in most counties, but only a few take junior members. You can find details of them from your local museum. Young people of 9 to 16 interested in taking an active part in archaeology should join 'Junior Rescue'. It costs 50p a year, and details of its activities are available from Mrs Kate Pretty, New Hall, Cambridge.

SOME BOOKS

There are a number of books on prehistory written for young people and amongst the most useful are:

Prehistoric Britain Barbara Green and Alan Sorrell (Lutterworth)

Prehistoric Britain Robin Place (Longmans)

Age by Age Ronald Jessup and Alan Sorrell (Michael Joseph)

Life in the Old Stone Age Charles Higham (Cambridge)

The Making of Man Ian Cornwall (Phoenix)

Ancient Britons M. M. Howard, H. Hodges and E. Pyddoke (John Baker)

The First People on Earth John Boddington (Hamlyn)

Archaeology Francis Celoria (Hamlyn)

The Young Archaeologist Leonard Woolley (Nelson) (This book is out of print but well worth trying to get from your Library)

Amongst many adult books that you will find interesting are:

Early Man F. Clark Howell (Time-Life)

Man the Toolmaker Kenneth Oakley (Natural History Museum)

The Neolithic Revolution Sonia Coles (Natural History Museum)

Pre-Roman Britain Stanley Thomas (Studio Vista)

Prehistory Derek Roe (Paladin)

Approach to Archaeology Stuart Piggott (Pelican)

Testimony of the Spade Geoffrey Bibby (Collins)

Collins Field Guide to Archaeology Eric S. Wood (Collins)

Discovering Archaeology in England and Wales (James Dyer (Shire)

Books about special areas of Britain:

Discovering Regional Archaeology series (Shire)
North-eastern England, North-western England, Central England, Eastern England, The Cotswolds and Upper Thames, Wessex, South-western England, South-eastern England, Wales.

Regional Archaeology series (Heinemann)
The Severn Basin, North Wales, South Wales, Yorkshire, South-west Scotland, Wessex, East Anglia, South-east Scotland.

Archaeology of Exmoor L. V. Grinsell (David and Charles)

Archaeology of Sussex E. C. Curwen (Methuen)

Archaeology of Cornwall Charles Woolf (Bradford Barton)

Archaeology of Wessex L. V. Grinsell (Methuen)

A Guide to Prehistoric England Nicholas Thomas (Batsford)

Southern England: an Archaeological Guide James Dyer (Faber)

Wales: an Archaeological Guide Christopher Houlder (Faber)

Finally, a popular magazine for anyone interested in archaeology:

Current Archaeology, published six times a year at a cost of £1.50 per annum and available from 9 Nassington Road, London, NW3 2TX.

Index

Abinger Common 26
Acheulean tools 19–20
Addedomaros 75
Aerial photography 17
Aichbühl 42
Animals 18, 22, 24–6, 27, 58, 62, 64
Arrows and archery 22, 44–5, 54, 68
Art 41, 58, 70–1
Astronomy 46, 48, 54
Atrebates 72–3
Avebury 36–7, 46
Axe factories 33–4
Axes, metal 50, 59, 61, 63, 68
Axes, stone 15, 27–8

Bank barrow 37
Barrows 13, 37–40, 48, 52, 54, 56, 58, 69
Baskets 34, 75
Beakers 44–6
Beaker Folk 44–50, 54
Belgae 72–7
Boats 26, 75
Bows and arrows 22, 44–5, 54, 68
Brochs 75–7
Bronze 46, 50–2, 57, 59–62
Bronze Age 14, 50–61
Burials 20, 23, 37–41, 44–5, 48, 52–56, 68–9, 75

Caesar, Julius 73, 77
Camulodnum (Colchester) 72–5
Cannibalism 69
Carts 62
Catuvellauni 73–7
Causewayed camps 35–7
Caves 19–20, 22
Cave pictures 22–3

Celts 70
Chariots 69, 73
Clacton 20, 22
Climate 24
Clothes 22, 23, 55–6, 69
Cogidubnus 73
Coins 73–5
Collared urns 50, 57
Copper 45–6
Cremation 39, 52, 57, 59, 72
Creswell Crags 23
Cunnington, William 12–13
Cup-and-ring marks 58
Cursuses 39

Disease, medicine 41, 54, 56
Dogs 26, 63
Drink 63
Druids 72
Dykes 68

English Channel 24
Entrance graves 41
Excavation 13–17

Farming 27–8, 57–60, 62–4, 75
Fields 58, 60, 62
Fire 22, 25, 63
Flint mines 30–3
Flint tools 19–22, 58
Funeral feasts 40

Glastonbury 63–4, 75
Goddesses 69
Gold 50–1
Grain 27, 58–9, 63
Grimes Graves 30
Grimspound 60

Handaxes 20–2
Henge monuments 35–7, 46
Hillforts 64–8, 72, 75
Hoare, Sir Richard 12–13
Homes 26, 28, 42–4, 57–60, 62–4

Homo sapiens 19–20
Ice Ages 18–19, 24
Initiation ceremonies 23
Ireland 40–1, 50, 58
Iron Age 14, 62–7
Itford Hill 57–8

Jewellery 50–1, 56–8, 68
Junior Rescue 78

Köln Lindenthal 42

Lamps, lighting 30
La Tène 66
Little Woodbury 63
Long barrows 37–40

Magic 22–3, 69
Maglemosians 25
Maiden Castle 37, 66
Megalithic yard 48
Men 18–20, 41, 44, 54
Mesolithic 24–6
Metal, metal working 45, 59, 69
Microliths 25–6
Middens 26
Mirrors 69–70
Mortuary huts 37
Museums 13–15, 78

Neanderthal man 19–20
Neolithic 27–49
New Grange 41

Old Stone Age 18–24

Palaeobotanists 24
Palaeolithic 18–24
Parisi 69
Passage graves 40–1
Paviland cave 23
Pitt-Rivers, A. 14
Ploughing 58, 62
Pottery 34, 39, 42, 44–5, 57, 63, 68, 72–3, 75

Prescelly Mountains 46
Pygmy cups 50–1

Querns 58–9, 63

Radio-carbon dating 15, 33
Religious sites 35, 40, 69
Rinyo 42
Rock shelters 19, 22
Romans 72–7

Scotland 40, 42, 46, 75
Severn-Cotswold tombs 39–40
Shearplace Hill 59–60
Silbury Hill 48
Skara Brae 42–3
Slaves 75
Sling warfare 68
Springs 69
Star Carr 25
Stone Age 14
Stone Circles 46–9
Stonehenge 37, 39, 46–7, 51, 52–4
Stratigraphy 16–17
Surgery 54, 56
Swanscombe skull 19

Thomsen, Christian 13
Trackways 28–30, 58
Traps 22
Tribes 68

Verulamium (St Albans) 72–3
Villages 30

Weapons 22, 50–2, 54, 57, 59–60, 68, 69, 72
Weaving 63, 77
Wessex culture 50–4
West Kennet long barrow 38–9
Wheel 62, 69, 73
Windmill Hill 35
Worsaae, Jan 14